MOSCOW ART NOUVEAU

MOSCOW ART NOUVEAU

KATHLEEN BERTON MURRELL

PHILIP WILSON PUBLISHERS

ACKNOWLEDGEMENTS

I am deeply indebted to Russian friends over the years for constantly encouraging and helping me in my increasing fascination with and discovery of the many and varied Art Nouveau buildings in Moscow. In particular I would like to mention Natasha Safontseva, a dedicated restorer of Moscow's crumbling buildings and a fervent admirer of the architect, Fyodor Shekhtel. It was she who was the impelling force behind this book and I thank her warmly. Sergei Romaniuk, the Moscow historian, as always generously gave me the benefit of his wide knowledge of Moscow buildings and gently advised me when I embarked on a wrong path.

In Britain, my old Moscow friend of long standing, Kate Cook-Horujy, gave her usual sage and sympathetic advice and spent much time ferreting out odd and useful facts. The architectural historian, Dr Catherine Cooke, whose expert studies of Moscow architecture of the early 20th century has been invaluable, kindly assisted in obtaining rare photographs. John Freeman, the photographer, has been more than generous in allowing the use of some of his wonderful Moscow interiors. Finally, I am very grateful to the principal photographer of the book, Igor Palmin, for his skill, patience and persistence in providing just the right illustrations.

© 1997 Philip Wilson Publishers Limited,
First published in 1997 by
Philip Wilson Publishers Limited
143-149 Great Portland Street
London W1N 5FB

Distributed in the USA and Canada by
Antique Collectors' Club Limited
Market Street Industrial Park
Wappingers' Falls NY 12590
USA

ISBN 0-85667-488-5

Editor Sally Prideaux
Designed by Sara Robin

Printed and bound in Italy by
Società Editoriale Libraria per azioni, Trieste

CONTENTS

INTRODUCTION

If the wasteland of suburban tower blocks that crowd suffocatingly around the old centre of Moscow is ignored, and only the ancient inner city is heeded, then a pleasant surprise is in store for the visitor. For, although some of the main arteries have been hacked about and made into bleak monuments to Soviet classicism, the lesser streets between the Sadovaya (Garden Ring) and the Kremlin are still lined with low private villas and charming apartment blocks of no more than five storeys built for the most part between the 1870s and 1914. Most of these buildings display to a greater or lesser extent the delightful mannerisms of Art Nouveau even if it is sometimes confined only to the facade where weirdly climbing plants spiral up the building or coloured tiles ingeniously attract the eye. The visitor must look beyond the peeling stucco walls to examine the variegated bentwood windows and see strange plants, grinning elves or serenely smiling ladies. For Moscow was largely rebuilt as the 19th century turned into the 20th and Art Nouveau, the style adopted by the merchant proprietors, became the imprint of the period not in just a few buildings here and there but for the central city as a whole.

Moscow in the early years of the 20th century was in a ferment of change; social, economical and political. Members of the landed aristocracy were caught in a long and painful decline while the merchants, newly enriched as industry rapidly expanded and now in control of the Duma, the city legislature, were faced with governing the rapidly growing city, a task their limited patriarchal outlook left them poorly equipped to do. Education gradually spread so that the illiterate peasant factory workers of the 1880s had become by 1905 a more politically aware proletariat seething with anger at poor wages and long hours and troops had to be called in to quell the disturbances. The riots led to short-lived political concessions, soon followed by reaction and repression which eventually, helped by the upheavals of the First World War, exploded in the revolution of 1917.

The pre-eminence of Art Nouveau in architecture was an interlude, a fleeting fashion, that would not nor could not last beyond the decade of its reign. It was more than just the rich merchant's penchant for something new and individual, although that was certainly part of its success. It also expressed the creative architect's striving for something new after the years of eclecticism that had dominated the last half of the 19th century.

Like his fellows in western Europe he wanted to create something more honest and innovative than facades copied from those of Italy or France disguising the rest of the building. The new technology just coming into use assisted him in achieving this ambition, for the wider use of glass, the freedom offered by reinforced concrete, and the strength of metal allowed him to make forms in almost any shape he desired. The new style offered unprecedented opportunities for experimentation and represented a vital step in the evolution of modern architecture.

The best of the Russian architects were well aware of the growth of Art Nouveau in Austria and Belgium and France through frequent travels and imported journals although it is not until the early 1900s that Russian architectural journals, which were then in their infancy, began discussing these developments. And in Russia, a distinctive offshoot of Art Nouveau appeared based on the colourful forms of early Russian architecture which had evolved away from direct western influences. Clearly Art Nouveau in Russia did not blindly emulate what was going on in western Europe but occurred spontaneously, in a parallel progression, influenced by many of the same social and aesthetic forces that affected the phenomenon elsewhere.

That this fact has not been generally known about Moscow is largely because of the almost complete silence on the subject by Soviet architectural historians and art critics who were brought up to despise the merchants as corrupt, oppressive and culturally ignorant. This prejudice extended to the buildings they sponsored and it is remarkable that those interested in the history of architecture could ignore such an integral part of the city landscape for so long. Finally, in the early 1970s a few trailblazing Soviet studies of Art Nouveau began to appear written by some remarkable pioneers in the field of whom Elena

Borisova, Tatiana Kazhdan, Professor Vladimir Kirillov and especially Evgeniya Kirichenko, with her excellent 1973 biography of Fyodor Shekhtel, led the way. One outstanding architectural historian of the 1960s, Professor Mikhail Ilin, in his 1963 architectural guide, *Moskva*, explained carefully 'Until recently we encounter in literature only negative attitudes to this style [Art Nouveau] evoked by the capriciousness, haphazardness and vagueness of some of its decorative motifs and techniques, which often prevented the architects concerned from achieving great, genuine art'. Nevertheless he boldly included a description of Shekhtel's masterpiece, the Ryabushinsky mansion (see pp 37-47), perhaps the most interesting of the Art Nouveau villas in Moscow, but felt obliged to add 'The Ryabushinsky mansion, the clearest and most consummate work of moderne [Art Nouveau], expresses with all its positive and negative features the cultural contradictions of bourgeois society.' Even as late as 1991 one respectable Moscow guidebook derisively refers to Art Nouveau architecture as 'capricious and mannered' or as merely a 'fanciful advertisement' for the merchant-owner. But today remarks such as these seem alien and out of date in a city now recognised as containing some of the finest Art Nouveau architecture in the world.

7

CHAPTER ONE
HARBINGERS OF THE 'STYLE MODERNE'

The birthplace of Art Nouveau in Russia is some sixty kilometres north of Moscow in lush, rolling countryside watered by innumerable small rivers and bounded by thick woods. It is here that a modest white-washed church has the honour of being the first creation of the 'Style Moderne' in Russia (1). The estate of Abramtsevo, where a sprawling single-storey wooden house set amid quaint buildings over-looks the Vorya River, seems at first sight the typical summer residence of a gentleman of means at the end of the 19th century. In 1874 it was purchased by the heir to a railway fortune, Savva Mamontov, and his wife, Elizaveta. Mamontov's main interest in life was not his increasingly lucrative business but opera and music and the visual arts. He and his wife had travelled extensively in Europe and stayed a while in Italy where they had become friendly with a group of prominent Russian artists under one of whom, Mark Antokolsky, Savva studied sculpture. On their return to Russia the hospitable Mamontovs created a remarkable focus for their interest in the arts by transforming Abramtsevo into a lively commune of the artists they had met in Italy and France plus many others. The gifted brotherhood was to endure for over twenty years and profoundly influenced the exuberant flowering of the arts in Russia in the first decade of this century. The artists Polenov, Serov, Repin, the Vasnetsov brothers, Vrubel, and the bass Chaliapin who was a discovery of Mamontov's, Stanislavsky and other luminaries all became part of the intimate community. The long summer sojourns of this galaxy of talent were taken up with experiments in art and design, the staging of specially written operas and plays, serious research into the history of Russian art and architecture, intense creative work in the ceramics studios and in the fields of embroidery and woodwork including furniture joinery. It was a true fusion of all the arts. The artistic experiences at Abramtsevo not only laid the foundations for the burst of creativity in the first decades of the 20th century but stimulated the revival of Russian arts and crafts that was to have far-reaching consequences within Russia comparable to that of William Morris and the Arts and Crafts movement in Britain.

ABRAMTSEVO CHURCH

Architecture figured large among the many achievements of the colony at Abramtsevo although there were no prominent architects among the group. Their most enduring creation is the enchanting Church of the Saviour Untouched by Hand (Nerukotvorny) (1). Completed by the whole group working together in 1882, it is a balanced asymmetrical reworking of early Russian historical styles in the manner of Philip Webb's free interpretation of the Gothic in his seminal 1860 Red House for William Morris. The Abramtsevo church is considered to be the first building of Russian Art Nouveau although it antedates the general emergence of the new style by nearly twenty years.

In the summer of 1880 a heavy spring flood prevented the Abramtsevo peasants from getting to the church in the Khotkovo convent five kilometres away to attend Easter service. This event inspired the deeply religious Elizaveta Mamontova to propose the building of a church on the estate. The community of artist friends seized on the idea with delight and immediately dedicated themselves to the new task. After intensive study and visits to the simple early churches of Yaroslavl and Rostov, and research into the 11th to 15th century buildings of Novgorod and Pskov, a plan was drawn up. The artist, Vasily Polenov (1844-1927), made the first sketches based on the Church of the Saviour Nereditsa in Novgorod, but Victor Vasnetsov (1848-1926), an artist of historical subjects who dabbled in architecture (see his Tretyakov Gallery, pp 87-90) modified the design allowing for elements of Moscow, Pskov, and Vladimir-Suzdal architecture to be woven in. It is the brilliant adaptation of features of these early churches, the precursors to the tower churches and baroque of the 16th and 17th centuries, which make this first neo-Russian, Art Nouveau building so original and revolutionary. The dome looks Pskovian, the bells hang above the western entrance like an old belfry (*zvonnitsa*), a frieze rings the cornice as in the old Moscow style, coloured tiles like those of Yaroslavl decorate the drum, and buttresses lean in on three sides. Decoration is limited to windows and doors, the frieze and the jutting apse. The interior is dominated by the elaborately carved and painted iconostasis which was created by all the artists working together (2). The floor, an

undulating sunflower, was designed by Vasnetsov who himself helped lay the tiles. Mikhail Vrubel (1856-1910), the most original and gifted of the artists, contributed the elaborately tiled stove (3). In 1892 a picturesque chapel was added to the north wall to contain the body of Mamontov's son, Andrei (4), and Mamontov himself was buried there at his death in 1918. The Abramtsevo church, a product of the inspired synthesis of the ideas of the whole community of artists working together, is the first Russian building based on

1 Vasnetsov and others, Church of the Saviour Untouched by Hand at Abramtsevo, 1882: the first Art Nouveau building in Russia.

2 Abramtsevo church: the unusually bare interior is adorned only by the carved and hand-painted iconostasis and Vasnetsov's sunflower floor.

traditional styles to avoid the pitfalls of too literal an interpretation, the so-called pseudo-Russian style.

Although some time was to elapse before the revolutionary ideas expressed in the Abramtsevo church were taken up, there is no doubt that the visionary design had immense significance for the next generation of Russian architects. Further afield, when the little church at Abramtsevo was being built, the European pioneers in Art Nouveau had scarcely begun. Victor Horta in Brussels was only beginning to debate the idea of a new architecture; Otto Wagner had not yet built his first suburban villa; Josef Olbrich was a school boy, and it was over a decade before Henry van de Velde designed the interiors of the Paris shop which inspired the name of the new architecture, 'L'Art Nouveau'.

DERIVATION OF ART NOUVEAU

Art Nouveau (Jugendstil, Secessionsstil, Stil floreale, Style Moderne) as it was expressed in architecture is not easy to define yet it is immediately recognisable by its distinctive ornament and unusual form. At the end of the 19th century designers, architects and artists in Europe and America were reacting against the academic classicism and eclectic mixing of styles that characterised the latter half of the century. In England and Russia they also turned away from the literal application of historical styles, the Gothic in the case of England and the pseudo-Russian (usually based on Moscow baroque of the 17th century) in the case of Russia, and set out to make something new and modern. The essence of Art Nouveau was first and foremost its ornament, the adaptation of traditional forms to create a new order, the free arrangement of space and the use of new materials. It is associated with the curved or geometric line based on floral ornamentation, or sometimes purely abstract lines, which can be highly exaggerated, disobeying traditional rules of construction. For example, the floral line can run up the entire height of a building continuing even beyond the cornice, in a manner unknown in Russian buildings since medieval times. The rules of symmetry can also be violated and two halves of a facade can differ extravagantly or bulbous extensions or towers may jut out in unexpected places. New materials which became technologically feasible at the end of the 19th century – iron, steel, glass and reinforced concrete – were incorporated into the composition of the new buildings releasing them from the usual construction restraints and allowing the freedom of greater internal spaces without visible supports. Finally, the union of art with architecture was an important element; the artist's conception would become as much a part of the building as the architect's. So the employment of coloured tiles became widespread, great panels of weather-proof mosaics embellished buildings, internal ceilings were richly painted or executed in relief, and stained glass enhanced the painterly effect.

3 Vrubel: the stove-bench in the main house at Abramtsevo, an example of his work in the ceramic studios in the 1890s.

4 Vasnetsov, 1891: the design for the chapel addition to the Church of the Saviour built to contain the body of Mamontov's invalid son, Andrei.

BACKGROUND – MOSCOW IN THE 19TH CENTURY

Architectural fashions reflect social and political history remarkably closely, a phenomenon no less true in Russia in the last century than in western Europe over the same period. Indeed, the architectural histories of Russia and of western Europe in the 19th century parallel each other to an exceptional degree. In Moscow architectural design moved through a long assured classical phase linked to the continued ascendancy of the nobility and the self-confidence of the Russian Empire which had defeated Napoleon in 1812, changing in the more unsettled period of the 1840s to an eclectic mixture, which in turn, as in western Europe, served to inaugurate the search for a new, assertive style. Coincidentally, a new awareness of the distinctive features of Russian traditional architecture emerged and the small churches and houses – *palata* – of the 17th century began to inspire those seeking a new style. The fashion for this indigenous style, so different from any western European models, is broadly parallel to the revivalist Gothic that overwhelmed Britain in the 19th century. It also reflects the polarisation of educated Russians into the Slavophiles, those who venerated Russia before the reforms of Peter the Great, and the Westernisers who exalted the culture and technology of western Europe. The use of traditional Russian medieval forms, encouraged in the 1830s and 1840s by Tsar Nicholas I, received great impetus in the second half of the century when major public buildings,

The striving for individuality was to doom the style from its inception and spell its death knell. But the short period of time from 1900 to 1910 in which Art Nouveau reigned was an extremely favourable moment for architecture since nearly everywhere in Europe a great building boom was going on. This was even more the case in Russia than in other countries and the large number of well-constructed buildings erected at that time in the central parts of Moscow have mostly survived in spite of Soviet waves of reconstruction and seventy years of neglect. They still dominate the old city within the Garden Ring road.

particularly in Moscow, were dressed in the conspicuous motifs of ancient Russia. However, it was to be some time before a true understanding of Russian medieval architecture would lead to a synthesis of the old styles in buildings such as the church at Abramtsevo.

Russia, an accepted partner of Europe after the shared experience of the Napoleonic wars, nevertheless differed from its western allies in two important ways, both with the continuing stranglehold of serfdom which oppressed seventy percent of the Russian population, and the associated backwardness of the economy. Emancipation of the peasants in 1861 by Alexander II not only removed the fetters of serfdom, it gave an impetus to the economy which in spite of problems such as the heavy debt incurred by the peasants to their former masters, began to grow at an astonishing speed. Although the low level from which the economy had to emerge must be taken into consideration, in the 1890s Russian industrial output as a whole grew at eight percent a year, faster than the economy of the United States, and by 1914 Russia had become the fourth largest industrial power in the world, ahead of France.

Moscow was undeniably well placed to take advantage of the industrial boom. It was not only the commercial, trading and financial heart of the country but also the geographical centre where water routes and the new railway lines converged, an advantage not shared by the capital, St Petersburg out on a limb in the Baltic Sea. Moscow was second only to St Petersburg

in the number of manufacturing industries and with emancipation, the problem of cheap labour was instantly solved. Peasants could at last freely leave the land and, succumbing to the irresistible temptation of paid work, flocked in their thousands to the cities, living without their families in crowded and unhygienic hostels. The great flow of labour into the city meant that, like St Petersburg, Moscow experienced a huge increase in population – the first census of 1871 reported 602,000 inhabitants but by 1899 the population had nearly doubled to over one million. Moscow at the turn of the century was a boom city, wide open for redevelopment, providing unparalleled opportunities for aspiring architects of the new style. A guidebook of 1895 published for the second congress of Russian architects, stated: '...Moscow has significantly altered its physiognomy. In this comparatively short period (twenty years) some parts of the city have become completely unrecognisable.'

RISE OF THE MERCHANT CLASS

Emancipation also drove a further nail into the coffin of a nobility already in decline, and gave a sharp boost to the rising merchant class. The new businessmen, who responded to the boom conditions of the second half of the 19th century, nearly all came from humble origins and many were of the stubborn and tenacious Old Believer sects known for their predilection for hard work. In the late 18th and early 19th century the more far-sighted serfs on the large estates that circled Moscow were able by dint of hard work and

5 Pavel Kharitonenko, the sugar merchant, with his wife, Vera, *circa* 1900.

6 Ton, Church of Christ the Saviour, 1837-83: the huge neo-Byzantine church, destroyed by the Soviets, is being rebuilt for the 850th anniversary of the founding of Moscow.

Nouveau suited them not only for its daring and modern approach but because it so clearly distinguished them from the nobility who were identified with the classical style. The merchants, who liked to build large extravagant houses adjacent to their factories even secretly including banned Old Believer chapels, were a great contrast to the serene and idle aristocrat in his columned mansion, who considered himself the arbiter of good taste, and who lived on the wealth gleaned from the land of estates which he rarely visited. The new merchant was usually landless, cunning and resourceful, conservative and autocratic. Even in his physical features he differed markedly from the tall, slim aristocrat tending to be stocky and small of stature, bullet-headed, with closely cropped hair (see, for example, the portraits (5 and 43) of Pavel Kharitonenko or Savva Morozov).

agreement of their masters to purchase their freedom and, with time, that of their families. They would set up small enterprises, perhaps selling handmade ribbons, and then by degrees move into the more lucrative Moscow market. The great textile families, the Tretyakovs and the Morozovs began in this way. Their descendants by the second and third generation were no longer so obsessed as their forebears with building up their businesses and many became generous patrons of the arts amassing superb collections of paintings or involved themselves in municipal politics.

These wealthy merchants, only one or two generations away from bonded serfdom, became important patrons of the new architecture. Art

By the second half of the 19th century Moscow was governed by the Duma, under a mayor or *golova*, who was usually a prominent merchant. The council members were practical men, rather like the Victorians, who understood the need for drains and clean water and these important amenities at last began to appear in the unsanitary city. They were less successful in attempting to assuage the staggering problems of the poor which could no longer be ignored in a city bursting at the seams. The city fathers decreed that factories had to be located beyond the Garden Ring road which formed the boundary of old Moscow thus protecting the centre with its magnificent fortress, the Kremlin,

the financial institutions of Kitai-gorod, and
the residential and shopping districts, from the
poorer areas where the former serfs, mostly men
with ties to their village, lived and worked in
appalling conditions.

BIRTH OF THE PSEUDO-RUSSIAN STYLE

By the 1840s the classical style was on the decline,
vulgarised and impoverished by the triumph of
eclecticism. At the behest of Nicholas I, a vast
cathedral was erected in Moscow, 1837-83, by
Konstantin Ton (1794-1881) to commemorate
the Russian victory over the French in the 1812
war. The huge Church of Christ the Saviour (6)
was designed in a bastardised version of the
Byzantine style mixed with poorly understood
references to Russian medieval architecture,
all on a vast and uncomfortable scale that
overwhelmed the ancient Kremlin nearby
(destroyed in 1931, it was rebuilt in 1997 for the
850th anniversary of the founding of Moscow).
Nicholas I's espousal of this building acted as a
spur to the adoption of the pseudo-Russian style,
romantic adaptations of pre-Petrine architecture
such as the florid Moscow baroque of the 17th
century. The momentous Polytechnic Exhibition
of 1872, the bicentenary of Peter the Great's
birth, also paradoxically encouraged the spread
of the pseudo-Russian style. The ambitious
exhibition which was the Russian equivalent of
Britain's Crystal Palace exhibition twenty years
earlier, had two superficially contradictory aims,
the first to revive interest in Russia's cultural

history – particularly costume, architecture and
art – and the second to demonstrate the
advantages of new technology from the west. In
both aims it was hugely successful; its exhibits
were subsequently used to found two new and
admirable museums, the History and the
Polytechnic. As Evgeniya Kirichenko says in
Moskva na Rubezhe Stoletii, 1977, p. 27: 'The
Exhibition of 1872 had a decisive significance
for the spread of the Russian style, which in
Moscow demonstrated surprising vitality.'

7 Shervud, History
Museum, 1874-83: the
spires and red brick were
intended to emulate those
of the Kremlin like the
Nikolsky Gate on the left.

Transformation of Red Square

Moscow's most ancient square outside the
Kremlin, Red Square, did not escape the mania
for reconstruction that characterises this period.
On two of its four sides striking new buildings
based on traditional Russian designs were
erected, the History Museum (7) and the Upper
Trading Rows (GUM), and just beyond the
Square the imposing Duma building, the city
legislature. They illustrate both the grandeur
and the limitations of the pseudo-Russian style.

History Museum

Count Alexei Uvarov of the Archaeological
Society and Professor Ivan Zabelin, the eminent
Moscow historian, headed the commission on
the construction of the new History Museum.
It was generally agreed that the design should be
based on traditional Russian architecture but the
Count and the Professor found it difficult to
agree which epoch or style should provide the
inspiration. The design finally chosen was not
only not by a professional architect but he was

8 Pomerantsev, Upper Trading Rows – GUM, 1889-93: the stone facade with its ancient Russian motifs is so lengthy it becomes tedious.

9 Upper Trading Rows – GUM: the great skylight illuminates one of the three elegant 'lines' of the arcade.

not even of Russian origin. Vladimir Shervud (Sherwood) (1833-1897), the Russian-born artist of British extraction, received the commission for the museum but his design did not please Professor Zabelin.

For Shervud, who as a student had been influenced by the Slavophiles including the writer, Nikolai Gogol, the position opposite St Basil's and flanking the Kremlin walls with their towers and merlons, was decisive in the final shaping of the scheme. He stated: 'In planning the design we considered it above all our duty to pay attention to the buildings already existing on Red Square, particularly the Church of St Basil the Blessed and the Kremlin walls and towers which would surround the History Museum and with which, therefore, it must find itself in accord.' (From Shervud's notebooks in the Russian Library quoted in Kirichenko, *Moskva na Rubezhe Stoletii*, 1977, p. 37).

The museum, constructed 1874-83, closing the narrower north side of the square, thus

11 Igumnov mansion: the entrance hall redolent of the garish claustrophobic chambers of the medieval terem palace in the Kremlin.

attempts to provide a foil to St Basils at the opposite, southern end, and to the Kremlin on its western flank. In this it could not succeed, for the forms and pinnacles of medieval Russian architecture mechanically applied to a balanced, symmetrical building of a later age inevitably look anomalous. Only when these forms are used in a free and imaginative way can they successfully be adapted to a modern building as was to be proved a short time later when some of the Art Nouveau architects fell under the spell of ancient Russia. Shervud's daring use of red brick in a reference to 17th century churches was an innovation in 19th century Moscow where the brick used in classical buildings was normally hidden under stucco impersonating stone. But

the museum, with its exaggerated towers and sloping roofs, is too replete with detail to be anything more than an indiscriminate collection of 16th and 17th century motifs. They are superimposed in a sterile fashion on a building the interior of which with its large well-lit halls is anything but medieval. Indeed, it is the interior of the History Museum, built by the outstanding engineer, Anatoly Semyonov, with its great collection of Russian artefacts and grand halls decorated by Vasnetsov and Semiradsky that is the more impressive. Yet the museum, in its wonderfully central position, is still easily the best of the three great pseudo-Russian public buildings constructed within a decade and a stone's throw of each other.

OPPOSITE
10 Pozdeyev, Igumnov mansion, 1893: the architect from Yaroslavl uses medieval motifs from his home town to great effect.

19

ABOVE
21 Savva Morozov mansion, 1893-98:
medieval motifs – crenellated roofs,
pinnacles and pointed arches – prevail
on the north, street facade.

LEFT
22 Savva Morozov mansion: the
quartered stained-glass window by
Mikhail Vrubel depicts the return
of a victorious knight lowering his
spear to receive garlands.

OPPOSITE
23 Savva Morozov mansion: the
vast stone and plaster fireplace
of the dining room designed by
Shekhtel exhibits an imagined coat
of arms. The furniture is original.

RIGHT
26 Savva Morozov mansion: the medieval mood is set by the snake and fierce dragon-like creature spitting at each other around the three-legged newel post.

OPPOSITE
27 Savva Morozov mansion: the grand main entrance hall is lit by the Tiffany lamp and the huge five-bayed window opposite.

34 Ryabushinsky mansion:
salamanders and lilies
contend for position
around the column of
the upper landing.

35 Ryabushinsky mansion:
the watery theme resonates
in the wave-like apertures
of the moulded staircase
and the newelpost lamp in
the form of a strange sea
creature with tentacles.

of the old faith and decorated their churches as they might have been in early 15th-16th century Muscovy. The four evangelists are shown allegorically on the pendentives that make the transition to the dome which represents heaven and is lit by a lantern skylight. The gilt design of the heavens and red pendentives are offset by the darker spiral pattern on the olive-green walls and by the stylised draperies painted traditionally on the lower part of Russian churches. These abstract patterns have something in common with the Art Nouveau designs of contemporary artists like the Swiss, Eugene Grasset.

In this fascinating chapel lies the spirit of the house, the successful combination of modernity and tradition. The Old Believer owners with their rigid domestic customs were dissidents from Orthodoxy and at the same time daring merchant businessmen not afraid to use the latest technology. It suited them to have a house of the newest, most advanced design by an architect who himself was not of the state religion, who was neither peasant nor aristocrat, but who was very much a part of the new society that had emerged at the beginning of the 20th century. This combination of far-seeing merchant and talented architect produced not only the most creative building of the early 1900s in Moscow but the most flagrantly outré chapel.

Survival in the Soviet Union

It is a tribute to Shekhtel's construction methods that the house has survived well and is now nearing its centenary. The Ryabushinskys emigrated after the 1917 revolution and the new Soviet government, as it did with all other private houses in Moscow, took over the mansion. It was given a variety of uses; first as the visa section of the new foreign ministry, then as the state publishing house (at this time the poet Yesenin described it as 'ultra-decadent'). In 1924 it became the fashionable Freudian Psychoanalytical institute for children but the institute was closed within a year and the director later arrested and sent to Stalin's camps. The house then became a nursery school for children of the Kremlin; Vasya, Stalin's son, was placed there. A year later it was returned to the foreign commissariat and became VOKS, the Society for Relations with Foreign Countries. It is not surprising to learn that the chairman, Olga Kameneva, the wife of Lev Kamenev and sister of Leon Trotsky, both leaders of the doomed left opposition to Stalin, was removed from her post in 1930 and imprisoned.

In the same year VOKS moved elsewhere and in May 1931 the mansion was given to Maxim Gorky, the writer, who returned home after his self-imposed exile in Italy. He had not been consulted as to his residence and did not appreciate the distinctive architecture, referring to it disparagingly as 'absurd'. He made a few unfortunate changes of which the most lamentable was the removal of the fireplace in the study and the concealment of the butterflies in the hall. Many writers visited him in this house including Romain Roland and George Bernard Shaw and, among Soviet visitors Stalin,

38 Derozhinskaya mansion, 1901-02: an archival photograph taken just after the house was completed.

who often called. Gorky died, possibly poisoned by Stalin, at his dacha in 1936 but his daughter-in-law, an artist, and his grandchildren continued to live there until his daugher-in-law's death. Today it is a museum both of its unique architecture, and of the last years of Gorky's life.

DEROZHINSKAYA MANSION

At the same time as Shekhtel was engaged on the Ryabushinsky house, and the pavilions for the Glasgow exhibition, he embarked upon his second epoch-making private mansion. Shekhtel, trained in the theatre and thoroughly accustomed to creating unusual visual effects, displayed his incredible versatility in this entirely novel dwelling, completely different from his earlier work, built 1901/02 in the Art Nouveau style (38).

The Butikovs

The client this time, Ivan Butikov, was not a high-ranking businessmen like the Ryabushinskys or a great mill lord like Savva Morozov but the owner of a small cotton factory. His business stood on the embankment of the Moskva River only a few blocks south of the new house he built for his daughter as an extravagant wedding

39 Derozhinskaya mansion: the monumental window of the principal projecting bay is framed behind the rotating triangles of the iron fencing originally repeated on interior furnishings.

present. His factory must have been successful for he was able to afford the services of Shekhtel, by then an architect at the height of fashion. Butikov's daughter, Alexandra, was marrying Derozhinsky, a senior officer in the Moscow police force and a graduate of the exclusive Corps de Pages in St Petersburg. As in other cases in Moscow, the title of the house remained with her. The marriage soon grew stale, and Alexandra discarded her policeman for Ivan Zimin, who with his brothers owned the large textile works in Zuyevo across the river from

Savva Morozov's large mill. Her new husband was brother of Sergei Zimin, the proprietor of the famous private opera in Moscow founded originally by Savva Mamontov of Abramtsevo. Derozhinskaya's marriages illustrate how the families of Moscow's mercantile society were intricately bound up with each other not only through artistic and commercial interests but also through their wives.

For Mrs Derozhinskaya-Zimina, Shekhtel built a highly imposing mansion. Whereas the Ryabushinsky house at Nikitsky Gates does not impress by its size but by its uniquely ornamented facade and interior arrangement, adornment is largely missing from the Derozhinskaya house. And whereas the Ryabushinsky house has at its centre the wonderfully sculptured staircase, in the Derozhinskaya the rooms revolve around a totally different axis, a giant medieval hall. In its lack of decoration, and the grand size of its hall, the Derozhinskaya house is clearly influenced by the Gothic style as the Morozov house so evidently was nearly a decade earlier. Yet it is so freely drawn, so uninhibited in the use of volume, so indifferent to earlier models, that its sheer originality leaves one gasping.

The Domesticated Castle

The house with its outbuildings, set back only slightly from the street, occupies nearly the whole plot leaving room only for a narrow garden. In the Shekhtelian manner, it is faced with glazed tiles of a light green colour which contrast with the cream-coloured stone dressings of the windows and doors (39). The wrought-iron fencing which divides it from the street is executed in a complex pattern of revolving triangles, a design which is repeated frequently within the house. The central projecting bay contains a giant-sized window that rises the full two storeys revealing the main feature of the house, the enormous hall within. Breaking through the roof line, it is surmounted by a strip of attic windows flanked by two round truncated towers, like the roof of a fortified castle. It thus presents a startling and unusual visage to the street, but its subdued colouring saves it from being aggressive.

The house is entered via the single floor vestibule from the driveway on the north. On the inner side of the door is a marvellous handle in the shape of a spider with long black legs. Brass hooks and cupboards provide space for storing the cumbersome winter clothing so necessary in Russia.

From the vestibule it is a few steps up to the central hall (41). Through double doors with brass handles that exhibit the same rotating triangles of the outside fencing is the great shell of the hall. It is truly medieval in size, its measurements an astonishing ten or twelve metres in width, length and height. The danger of a bleak and cold room is averted by the rich use of warmly coloured wood. The parquet flooring and the superb wooden panelling which rises halfway up the walls, are matched by a wooden coffered ceiling. It is impossible to furnish this room satisfactorily and Shekhtel

wisely left it almost bare. He did design special settees, though, that hung from the panelling rather than standing freely on the floor. Upholstery for the settees was in the familiar rotating triangle design, perhaps made at the Butikov factory. The present inhabitants have wisely left the parquet floor bare and installed a minimum amount of sitting room furniture.

40 Derozhinskaya mansion: the circular form of the staircase is repeated in the spirals of its iron railings.

ABOVE
44 Moscow Arts Theatre, 1902: Stanislavsky's
canon that theatre be unpretentious is admirably
fulfilled in the simple elegant lines and austere
decoration of the main auditorium.

OPPOSITE
45 Moscow Arts Theatre: one of the
public rooms decorated with cuboid
hanging lamps and the theatre's seagull
motif designed by the architect.

49 Moscow Arts Theatre: the functional lamp is offset by flowers on long stalks that flow languidly across the ceiling.

From Olga Knipper's letters to Chekhov we know that the company were thrilled at the prospect of not only a new specially designed theatre but the vastly improved conditions backstage. Because of the attention to the stage and new dressing rooms, the foyer had to be kept to a minimum, a narrow corridor as one enters with the usual cloakroom for leaving coats on the right. But several rooms for refreshments and for the inevitable promenading that Muscovites like to do in the intervals were provided. They were decorated in variations of the linear design that so distinguishes the rest of the building (45). Exclusively light colours were used – greeny-greys and off-whites – and the resulting plain walls were enlivened only by fine

OPPOSITE
48 Moscow Arts Theatre: the plain walls are enlivened only by a wavy design and dignified lettering announcing the dress circle.

59

gateway to the north advertising the new railway, a reminder of the architecture of the towns through which the line passed (50). Inspiration came not only from the wonderful wooden churches with their towers and the large wooden houses with their steeply pitched roofs, but the stone and brick forms and exotic ornament of the kremlins and monasteries of Yaroslavl and Vologda. He put it all together, added colour in the form of ceramic tiles made at Mamontov's workshop at Abramtsevo, and placed diverting reliefs of northern animals all over the upper reaches of the building. The effect, so unlike Stanislavsky's austere theatre, is bombastic, a shouting commercial for the delights and rich natural wealth of the Russian north. Contemporaries criticised it for being all facade and although Shekhtel was at pains to make a spacious and comfortable station hall within decorated with panels by the artist Konstantin Korovin (1861-1939), it is true that the exterior facing the square where two other railway stations compete for attention, was the more important.

By the time that Shekhtel began work on the construction of the station in 1902, Mamontov had suffered a terrible misfortune. In 1899 he was arrested for fraud and embezzlement and languished in prison for nine months. Although in July 1900 he was acquitted and released, his business had in the meantime failed. He was a ruined man and the railway line passed out of his hands. Nevertheless, the station was built by the new owners as he had commissioned it and

stands to this day, a witness to the powerful artistic convictions of one of the most farseeing Russians of the century.

The Facade

It faces the square belligerently, the high central gateway crowned by a looming roof embracing the two round turrets, so steeply pitched it resembles a high hat pulled over a forehead. Small gable windows peek out like visors from this headgear. At the apex wrought ironwork, inscribed with the initials for the USSR which replaced the original double-headed eagle, resembles that of a medieval Russian house. In the arch bas-reliefs of a fisherman, an Eskimo and the Soviet coat of arms long ago replaced the symbols of Arkhangelsk, Yaroslavl and Moscow – the Archangel Michael, the Bear and St George respectively. The walls are flanked by towers at either end, the one on the right with projecting machicolation supported by brackets like a fortress and finished by a tall tetrahedral roof. On the left the slimmer tower with its octagonal roof was used as a water tower. The whole building is replete with delightful reliefs and intaglio carvings of the animals and birds and plants – bears, and wolves and cormorants – that inhabit the wild and beautiful regions of Russia's north. But the ceramic polychrome tiles are the most expressive feature. In blues and greens and light browns they form a grand frieze below the roofline enhancing the brown brick walls and the white stucco of the detailing and portico arch and the tall dark roofs. Tiles also

flank the central portico depicting giant strawberries and flowers (51).

This ingenious piece of promotion makes no pretence at symmetry, reflecting the medieval love of the picturesque in architecture. The brilliant, exotic design, combined with wonderful craftsmanship and artistry, and enhanced by colour and sharply etched forms,

make the ordinary traveller to this day anxious to taste the delights of Vologda or Yaroslavl, Kostroma and Kargopol and Arkhangelsk. This most imaginative building, which surprises and confuses the foreigner, conveys to the Russian observer a clear picture of the architectural and natural beauties of the far mysterious north. It is pure theatre on a Moscow square.

51 Yaroslavl station: the huge strawberries and blue tiles made at the Abramtsevo studios frame the Soviet relief of the central arch.

ABOVE
52 Kekushev's first house,
1898-99: the tympanum
designed by William Walcot
of tiles prepared at the
Abramtsevo studios depicts
fish and flowers cavorting
in an underwater kingdom.

OPPOSITE
53 Kekushev's first
house: lightly glazed brick
with stone trim, moulded
arches, coloured tiles and
floral relief in the window
architrave characterise this
early Art Nouveau house.

stumpy columns of old Russia is abruptly cut out of the square of the first floor; the balustrading added later has spoiled the effect of the original dramatic gap between the columns. From this balcony when the house was built there would have been delightful views of the Kremlin and the monumental Church of Christ the Saviour. A fine mosaic in Abramtsevo ceramic tiles by the half-English architect, William Walcot (see pp 74-81) who developed this skill at the Mamontov studios, decorates the tympanum of the front entrance (52); other Abamtsevo tiles are placed to good effect under the windows where stylised flowers are cut out of the architraves. The interior is left plain except for the liberal use of wood panels and the doorway mouldings (54) and (55). The powerful grand staircase proceeds upwards alongside the plain

rusticated wall lit by a large landing window. The house is placed on rather a small plot, widening at an angle to the rear where, as in many town houses of this date, there is virtually no garden.

Second Kekushev House

Kekushev's second house on Ostozhenka completed two years later at the end of 1901 is much more vigorous in design than his first. It is composed of differing sections reflecting the interior arrangement of the rooms but these elements are harmoniously fused by such devices as the stone trim or repetitions of the central stylised pediment and the inventive flower design. The strange mansion is obviously inspired by medieval European chateau architecture but achieves its effect as much from the strongly moulded window and door frames, especially of the front porch, and the contrast between the brown brick of the walls and the cream stonework, as from the polygon tower of various floors with its octagonal tiled tent roof (56). The central pediment originally culminated in an arrogant and rather ridiculous standing lion, a play on Kekushev's first name, Lev (lion). The lion is now no more but the rest of the stonework survives well including the frieze of foliage under the eaves and in the cornice of the tower and the self-conscious pediment. Like other houses of this type, it is on a small lot, with no front garden, but at the back where the master's study was situated, it faces the once lovely Zachatiya Convent in a district of Moscow

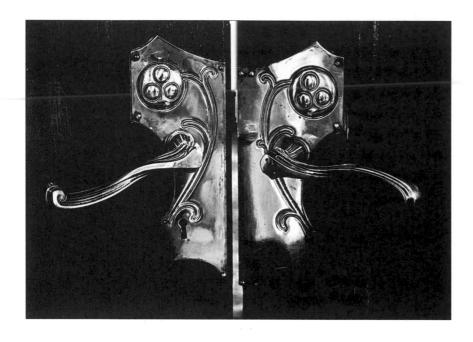

54 Kekushev's first house: intricate brass door handles enliven the interior rooms.

high-rises, is an unexpected discovery. Set back from busy Electrozavodskaya Street a comfortable, spacious two-storey house (No.12) welcomes the passer-by with a wide old-fashioned verandah. The way the verandah sweeps around three sides in a deep curve combined with the curving overhanging cornice and large, strongly-accentuated windows, makes it seem more appropriate for a country dacha or a comfortable house of an American small town, than this old district of Moscow (57).

The unusual house was built for Vasily Dmitrievich Nosov, the long-established wealthy textile manufacturer whose less remarkable main house of the mid 19th century is just next door at No.1, Zhuravliev Square, and whose textile mill was only a few blocks away. Moscow's merchants always preferred, if possible, to live near their factories in order to keep a watchful eye on the business. Nosov's son ,also called Vasily, incurred the wrath of his conservative parents when he married Efimiya Ryabushinskaya, sister of Nikolai and Stepan (see p. 40), of the extremely wealthy but, in their eyes, upstart merchant family. Efimiya was as enterprising as her brothers, however, and set out to amass an art collection that she hoped would rival even that of Pavel Tretyakov. Along with so many others, it was nationalised after the revolution but one suspects Efimiya would have approved for it was her stated intention ultimately to give the paintings to the nation. The collection includes several fascinating portraits of this beautiful headstrong woman by leading artists

that gently slopes to the river. Kekushev also designed the more restrained three-storey apartment building next door (east). His house was taken over by the Soviet Foreign Ministry after the revolution and was let to foreign emissaries, on the whole not the worst of tenants.

American Dacha

In the unfashionable east end of Moscow beyond the Yauza River, a tributary of the Moskva, the decaying houses of the few old streets that survive from a century ago are dominated by smoking chimneys and the noise of machines. It is hard to imagine Peter the Great as a child here in the large wooden ramshackle palace surrounded by fields and villages. But today, among the mills and factories built before and after the revolution and the clusters of modern such as Konstantin Somov and Alexander Golovin. She also had her house decorated by leading artists including the theatre designer, Mstislav Dobuzhinsky, who painted the strange ceilings resembling mosaics that still enthral the visitor to what is now the local district museum.

It was Vasily senior who, it seems, inspired by a picture of an American country cottage in the journal, *Scientific American* immediately invited Kekushev to create for him something similar next door to his Moscow house. Kekushev fulfilled the commission admirably. The house, built of wood on a brick foundation, and completed in only one year in December 1902, has indeed the artlessness and plasticity and comfort of an American suburban home. The rooms were centred around the staircase and the walls were prudently hung in textiles

or covered in oak panelling instead of the more expensive plasterwork. Sadly today the house has been much altered and spoiled after years as an institution and only the staircase, the fireplace and some of the doors survive of the original. But the exterior form is still undiminished and the verandah, the overhanging cornice, as well as the windows and carvings of the porch balustrades, still speak forcefully of the freshness of Art Nouveau.

Mindovsky Mansion

Of all Kekushev's impressive houses built for private clients, the best and most original is the one purchased by Ivan Mindovsky near the centre of Moscow at No. 44 Povarskaya, now the Embassy of New Zealand. It was built 1903-04 to Kekushev's design together with the

55 Kekushev's first house: an embossed panel in the principal salon.

57 Kekushev, American dacha, 1902: the rustic Nosov house, based on an American east coast country home, seems out of place surrounded by factories in Moscow's east end.

neighbouring No. 42 for a commercial building firm, the Moscow Trading and Construction Company, who demolished a large classical mansion to make way for the two profitable houses. The second house, also in Art Nouveau style but very different to Mindovsky's, was so heavily altered in 1914 that it is hard now to credit it with Kekushev's hand. The Mindovsky mansion, however, is well preserved and relatively unchanged. Like most of his houses, it is a simple cube placed on a narrow lot but invigorated with the rhythmic flowing lines of curves and arches,

projecting bays, and fine sculpture. At roof level the overhanging cornice swoops up and down with great effect in line with the dramatic curves of the bays (58). On the south-facing street corner a five-window bay with floor to ceiling windows encloses the fashionable winter garden (60). A woman's head peeks seductively over the main upper window on the street side, other figures sport under the eaves among more ordinary floral designs and medallions. Originally a tall figure of a mother and two small children stood on the curved gable above the

OPPOSITE
56 Second Kekushev house, 1901: the central pediment decorated in a foliage design like the tower was originally embellished with a watchful lion, a play on the architect's first name, Lev (lion).

61 Mindovsky mansion: lion's head on the bronze and marble staircase.

balcony but it has long since been lost. Like the Moscow Empire houses of an earlier time, it is entered from the courtyard through fine iron Art Nouveau gates that may be a little later than the interesting fencing as the design does not quite match. Unusually for Moscow, all the original service buildings in the courtyard which form an admirable counterpart to the house, are still in place.

The rooms within are less dynamic than one would expect from the splendidly sinuous exterior; indeed the sculptural frieze of the sedate staircase is distinctly classical and the bronze balusters are spaced with fine lions' heads (61), but the original doors (59), metal work, stained glass, the elegant sculptured ceiling of the dining room, and fireplaces survive and it has been redecorated tactfully in the original pastel colours of the time.

PHENOMENON OF WILLIAM WALCOT

The architectural world of turn of the century Moscow was greatly enriched by the unorthodox figure of William Walcot (1874-1943). He was born in Odessa to a peripatetic businessman father, Frank Walcot, of English nationality and to a Russian mother of German origin whose family had come to settle the colonies of New Russia in the late 18th century. Walcot spent his childhood with his wandering English father visiting western Europe and South America. There was little that was English in his early background for his education took place mostly in France, where he studied at the School of Fine Art in Paris and with the artist, Odilon Redon. He then moved to St Petersburg where he studied architecture under Leonty Benois, who was to tutor many of the leading architects of Walcot's generation. His experiences on his wide-reaching travels must have given him artistic insight into the new developments in the world of art in those heady days of impressionism and symbolism and the thrilling development of the arts and crafts movement. Indeed, in the mould of William Morris, he was as much a craftsman as an architect, for he designed furniture, and threw pots and made tiles, and in his latter years in England he became best known for his fine architectural drawings. In 1897 aged twenty- three the young man moved to Moscow, then in the middle of the great building boom, where opportunities for architects were almost unlimited. Walcot immediately entered the competition for the Metropole Hotel and

62 Walcot, Metropole Hotel, 1899-1905: the ceramic panel decorating the pediment was based on Vrubel's design of the *Princess of Dreams* made for the 1896 exhibition.

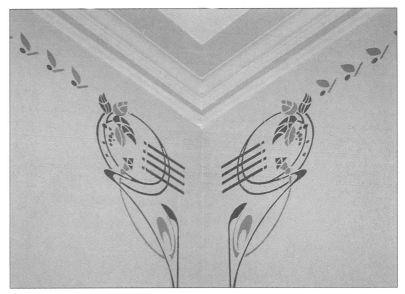

LEFT
63 Metropole Hotel: a detail of one Golovin's panels.

ABOVE
64 Metropole Hotel: one of the many fine Art Nouveau wall designs of the hotel restored in 1991.

exceptionally, the young, untried architect was successful; his very first building was one of the most important to be built in Moscow in the 1890s. His future career must have seemed assured but in 1906, owing to the illness of his wife, he left to spend the rest of his days in England. Although he stayed less than a decade in Moscow, he bequeathed an astonishingly diverse legacy of excellently conceived Art Nouveau buildings.

Metropole Hotel

The St Petersburg Insurance Society in 1896 announced a competition for a grand new hotel to be located in the centre of Moscow opposite the Bolshoi Theatre. It was to be the largest in the city with over four hundred rooms, and was to occupy an entire block (66). Kekushev was already involved in working out a plan to incorporate the 1830 walls of the old hotel into the new on the unusually shaped site where the back section abutted onto the ancient walls of Kitai-gorod. As a result of a disastrous fire in 1901 just as it was virtually ready, the Metropole was to take nearly seven years to build, from 1899-1905, and cost a staggering seven million rubles, more than double the amount forecast by the society.

Of the twenty entries considered by the jury, Walcot's came fourth (first prize was Kekushev's). But, because the head of the jury was Savva Mamontov, the owner of the Abramtsevo estate where the Russian arts and crafts revival was in full spate, Walcot's design was in the end adopted. Mamontov, who regarded the monumental building as a new cultural centre for Moscow, was keen to incorporate as much of the visual arts as possible and considered that Walcot's scheme allowed the greatest opportunity for sculptural, wrought ironwork, painting and ceramic embellishments. The building is thus heavily engaged in the upper parts both in the architectural and the ornamental sense, leaving the middle floors between the balconies bare except for the glass bays at the extremities and the centre. Although it could be argued that it is overladen with decorative devices, there is no doubt that the delightful sculpture and the ceramic panels enrich and

65 Mikhail Vrubel, the artist, about 1900. Vrubel worked with Shekhtel on several private houses and designed the ceramic panels that adorn the Metropole Hotel.

66 Metropole Hotel: the first luxury hotel in Moscow and the only one successfully to combine art, sculpture and architecture in one building.

distinguish the building. Around the upper third/ fourth floor window openings a relief on the theme of the seasons of the year executed by the leading sculptor, Nikolai Andreev (1873-1932), extends in a wide band around the building. Although the addition of the curving pediments greatly altered Walcot's original design, they provided backdrops for the large ceramic panels that are the most distinctive feature of the Metropole. The remarkable central panel which faces the main street, Teatralny Proezd, is by Mikhail Vrubel (65), the leading artist of the period (see also pp 28-30 and 32). Vrubel and Walcot were well acquainted with each other for the architect had spent some time under Vrubel's guidance learning ceramics at the studio at Abramtsevo. The panel (62) is taken from

Vrubel's painting of the *Princess of Dreams* based on Edmond Rostand's play, *La Princesse Lointaine*, which was popular on the Moscow stage at the time. When Vrubel had tried to display the panels at the famous Nizhny Novgorod fair of 1896, the shocked jury refused them entry. Undaunted, Mamontov, Vrubel's patron, ordered a special pavilion to be built just outside the exhibition grounds where the painting was shown to great acclaim. The *Princess of Dreams* has long been recognised as a masterpiece and is now in the Tretyakov Gallery, having found room at last with other monumental Vrubel paintings in the enlarged exhibition halls opened in 1994. Alexander Golovin (1863-1930), another artist associated with Abramtsevo, who worked in the theatre and was known as a fine ceramicist,

68 Yakunchikova mansion: one of the
bay windows displaying fine metalwork
and subtly coloured tiles made in the
Abramtsevo workshops.

67 Walcot, Yakunchikova
mansion, 1899-1900:
the strong right angles
and flat roof contrast
strongly with Walcot's
Gutkheil mansion next
door.

realised the panels which included besides the
Vrubel painting seven others of his own design
that look out onto three main sides of the
building (63). Walcot was also responsible
for the fine ironwork of the balconies and for
the courtyard gates.

At the roof line it is clear that Walcot was
aware of the historical position of the Metropole
for he complemented the battlements of the
Kitai-gorod walls that bordered the hotel when

it was built (a fragment survives still) with
pointed pinnacles and other superstructures on
the roof. At ground level the large archways
intended for shops intentionally reflect the
arches of the Maly Theatre opposite, the motif
which dominated the square when it was rebuilt
by Bove after the fire of 1812. It also repeats the
grand archway of the Tretyakov gateway into
Kitai-gorod on the east side. The interior too,
supervised by Kekushev and designed by

Vasnetsov, Erikhson and perhaps Shekhtel, was replete with sculptural reliefs, wall and ceiling ornament (64), stained glass and charming Art Nouveau lifts. The dining room and tea room were especially lavishly decorated. Oddly, the ceiling of the old entrance hall has the same relief pattern as Kekushev used in the Mindovsky mansion dining room and which he probably designed himself. Converted into offices for the Bolsheviks after the revolution,

the Metropole fell on hard times not relieved when it returned to use as a hotel again in the 1930s. In the mid-1980s a refurbishment and restoration plan under Russian restorers and Finnish builders, however, returned it to its former elegance, a first-class hotel, and one of the most beautiful in Europe. This was too early in the Perestroika period, however, for it to be seemly to erase from the facade the banal Lenin dictum: 'Only the dictatorship of the proletariat

69 Walcot, Gutkheil mansion, 1902: the symmetry and the light glazed brick of the facade blend well with the small, pastel-coloured 19th century houses of the district.

OPPOSITE
73 Solovyev, Medvedkova almshouse, 1902-03: the vast poorhouse and hospital was endowed with two chapels based on the ancient churches of medieval Russia.

BELOW
72 Ostrogradsky, City Primary School, 1909: the mosaic of St George and the Dragon adorns a model building for the increasing number of city schools.

ABOVE
71 Zelenko, 'Settlement' School, 1907: the lively building protrudes and recedes, extends upwards and inwards, reflecting the shape of the observatory, halls, theatre and workshops within.

development of the child. One of the pioneers in Russia, Stanislav Shatsky (1878-1934), propagated the idea of education through the application of labour. After the revolution Shatsky's ideas were taken up by the Bolsheviks and he became very influential in the educational reforms and experiments of the 1920s, and founder of the short-lived Labour Schools. By the 1930s when the Soviet Union eschewed progressive ideas, he fell from favour and was no longer influential.

Alexander Zelenko was also deeply interested in educational reform and in the early 1900s travelled the world studying educational movements in other countries, especially the ideas of John Dewey in the USA. In 1906, together with Shatsky, he founded the educational society 'Settlement' modelled on the American society of that name, whose stated aims were to form free schools of 'Children's Work and Leisure' where the elements of science and the arts would be imparted in a community spirit. Zelenko, full of enthusiasm, employed his considerable imagination to turn these new ideas into an appropriate and utterly different school building to be situated in the unfashionable area north of the Garden Ring road near the notorious Butyrki prison. It was completed in 1907. The construction and the running costs of the school were financed by subscriptions from sympathetic members of the intelligentsia. Throughout the rest of his life Zelenko continued to involve himself in educational problems as much as architecture. After the revolution he worked in

educational research and wrote many articles on the subject but like Shatsky, his pioneering work came to an end in the 1930s.

Today the strange, idiosyncratic building set slightly back from the street of dull shabby Soviet boxes of the 1960s and 1970s still startles the passerby. In sharp contrast with the other buildings on the street the school seems hardly to display a straight line, its sinuous outline resembling more a strange, growing plant from another galaxy. The various parts of the wonderfully moulded rough cast walls seem to flow and ebb organically in and out of each other, now round, now flat, now square now circular, moving horizontally and then vertically, revealing the complex interior of large halls, a theatre, the workshops and the glass-topped observatory tower. No other decorative device is used apart from the plasticity of the walls and the windows directed to the light. The variously grouped windows placed freely in an uninhibited fashion clearly identify the rooms inside; the stepped windows indicate the staircase, the large windows show the large halls, the smaller the more intimate workshops. The variety in size and shape of window demonstrates the struggle between the contrasting elements; small versus large, vertical versus horizontal, round versus square. Small pre-school children aged four to six filled the school in the mornings while teenagers up to age seventeen used it in the late afternoons. The 130 children learned through their own efforts all manner of handicraft, music, drawing and sculpture, and even gymnastics and

were themselves encouraged to choose the activity. This remarkably progressive school for its time was closed after the revolution and the building, today in shoddy condition, was used as a Soviet children's palace of culture for which it is well suited.

City Primary School

Although nothing like as fanciful as Zelenko's school, an impressive new primary school on four floors was completed in 1909 by Anatoly Ostrogradsky (1872-?) for the city at Bolshaya Pirogovskaya 9. It was part of the huge programme to extend primary education to children begun after the reforms of 1860 by the city government, private welfare organisations and the orthodox church. In cities like Moscow and St Petersburg, the best could be compared to those in western Europe and America and by 1914 the city was able to boast that not one child of primary school age (eight-eleven) desiring to enter school, was turned away. The literacy rate in Moscow had risen so rapidly with the expansion of the school system that by 1914 nearly ninety percent of boys and seventy-four percent of girls aged twelve to twenty were literate compared to an

overall rate for the whole population of about fifty percent in 1897. The literacy rate for girls, which had been abysmally low, was the most remarkable improvement.

The school reflects the romantic revival of interest in the Russian past pioneered by the archaeologists and founders of the new national museums in the late 19th century as well as the influence of the arts and crafts movement at Abramtsevo. The model primary school on four tall floors has conspicuously large windows lighting the unusually spacious classrooms. Its patriotic decor illustrates the fashion for traditional Russian design in the use of gables and the large coloured mosaic by Sergei Chekhonin (1878-1936) of St George and the Dragon, the emblem of Moscow, which spreads across the eaves (72). This striking building, emblematic of the campaign to spread education in the early years of this century, is now no longer a school but a research institute.

Medvednikova Almshouse

In the course of only one year, 1902-03, a grand charitable complex was constructed in the south-west of Moscow on Bolshaya Kaluzhskaya

74 Solovyev, 1901-02: relief of a stalking lion by Nikolai Andreev at the doorway to Solovyev's own house.

(Leninsky Prospekt) across from the royal palace of Neskuchny Sad and near the large Golitsyn hospital. This was a popular district for benevolent institutions and from the 1880s to the outbreak of the First World War whole complexes of orphanages, poor houses, hospitals and special schools were established on this and parallel streets. They were founded by well-meaning wealthy citizens, mostly members of the merchant guilds, for whom public charitable acts took on almost the character of a fashion. One such citizen, Alexandra Medvednikova, the widow of a rich factory owner, died in 1899 on her estate at Poreche southwest of Moscow (later to become a special sanatorium of the Moscow branch of the communist party). She generously willed the then huge sum of two million rubles to the city for the building and maintenance of a poorhouse, a hospital for the chronically and mentally ill, and for the elderly. There was even a sum set aside to cover the running costs of the establishment.

Sergei Solovyev (1859-1912), the architect for the complex, took as his model the unique architecture of medieval Russia before it was 'corrupted' by the westernising reforms of Peter the Great, and adapted it to the modern building (73). The result is a delightfully picturesque version of the 12th-15th century Novgorod/ Pskov styles, highly exaggerated in the Art Nouveau manner.

The *bogodelnya* or almshouse extended over a large territory flush with the busy main road, Bolshaya Kaluzhskaya (later Leninsky Prospekt)

with the poorhouse on the left, which also bears the name of another donor, A.K. Rakhmanova, and hospital on the right, each with their own chapel at the centre. Buildings containing apartments for doctors and nurses were built deep in the courtyard in the space between the two institutions. The long two-storey buildings with large windows are especially well lit. The hospital was built with sunny south-facing wards and unusually bright corridors, which widened at the centre into day clinics and concluded at the extremities in attractive hexagonal rooms. At the point where hospital and poorhouse meet, the two chapels named for particular icons of the virgin, stood at right angles to one another. Asymmetrical in volume and of varied height, each has its own small cupola on a slim drum and each flourishes an attractive roof belfry (73). That of the hospital chapel is especially charming with three cupolas closely grouped over the central of the three bell apertures. The decorative forms of medieval Russia are skilfully deployed in the picturesque porches, in the *begunets*, chevron-like bands and in the *shirinki* or indented squares.

After the revolution, the charity institutions were closed, and in 1923 the buildings were taken over to become city hospital No. 5 and the chapels shut down. In 1992 the hospital was reorganised as the central hospital of the Moscow Patriarchate and the chapels, used as hospital departments, were rededicated under the names Alexei, Metropolitan of Moscow, and the Tikhvin Icon of the Holy Virgin.

NEO-RUSSIAN VARIANT

The most individual manifestation in Russia of Art Nouveau was the neo-Russian style already encountered in connection with the Abramtsevo church (pp 8-12), Shekhtel's Yaroslavl station (pp 60-63), the Medvednikova almshouse (pp 83 and 85-86) and Ostrogradsky's City Primary School (pp 82 and 85). The particular popularity of neo-Russian among client and designer derived from its capacity to be both modern in the use of the new technology and at the same time patriotic in the way it harked back, as it seemed to those fearful of the effects of the industrial age, to a more innocent era.

By 1900 buildings in the neo-Russian manner began to sprout everywhere in Moscow, superseding the popular, but more literal 19th century pseudo-Russian style. Although both

75 Vasnetsov, Tretyakov Gallery, 1906: the stylised facade based on 17th century Russian architecture is a brilliant advertisement for Russia's primary collection of domestic art.

then a broad band of giant lettering on a white background giving the names of the donors, Pavel Tretyakov and his brother Sergei, and the City of Moscow. Above that is a further broad frieze of glazed Abramtsevo tiles. All this is interrupted at the centre by two sets of triple windows in black above which the traditional ogee-shaped gable breaks through the roof carrying a large bas-relief of St George and the Dragon, the emblem of Moscow. It is a supremely successful play on historic Russian themes, at once familiar and different, romantic and practical, embodying the spirit of neo-Russian Art Nouveau.

77 Pertsov apartment house: detail of one of the dragon corbels.

Over the years Vasnetsov's reconstruction proved inadequate for the growing collection and new additions to the gallery in Soviet times only provided temporary relief. Finally, in 1985 the Tretyakov was closed for complete reconstruction including the incorporation of neighbouring old buildings into one large gallery. During the massive rebuilding nothing survived of Tretyakov's original house but Vasnetsov's wonderful facade was saved. Renewed and enlarged, the gallery at last reopened ten years later, in 1995. Visitors still enter through the marvellous red and white portal that reminds them of Russia's past and prepares them for the feast of paintings beyond.

Pertsov Apartment House

Sergei Malyutin (1859-1937), also an artist but eleven years younger than Vasnetsov, entered the field of neo-Russian architecture with results almost as spectacular as those of the older painter. Like Vasnetsov, Malyutin played a prominent role in the revival of Russian crafts not at Abramtsevo but at the estate of Princess Tenisheva at Talashkino near Smolensk, where a community similar to the one at Abramtsevo was formed. Malyutin was in charge of the arts and crafts workshop there and also played an active role in theatre design and furniture making. In 1907 with the civil engineer and structural expert, Nikolai Zhukov (1874-1945), he designed the facade and decorated the interior floors and staircases of the apartment building of Zinaida Pertsova, on the Kremlin embankment near the massive Church of Christ the Saviour (76). Malyutin also designed the Pertsov's own apartment in the building in a florid romantic application of traditional designs reminiscent of the grandiloquent terem palace in the Kremlin. The tiled depictions of Russian folklore on the steeply pitched gables and around the windows of the upper part of the five-storey red brick building, and the sculptured figures and carving of the lower balconies and entrances where dragons (77) suddenly seem ready to breathe fire on the unwary passer-by, give the otherwise ordinary building the colour and drama associated with the theatre. The Pertsov house displays the blending of art and architecture that gives Art Nouveau its special value and it is no wonder that artists, including Kazimir Malevich, chose to live in this visually arresting house. Even after the revolution artists of the calibre of Robert Falk continued to live here. (In the 1980s the tenants were forced to leave so it could become an office block for foreign firms).

Only one other apartment house in Moscow also by an artist has a similarly worked facade although it lacks the colour of the Pertsov house. East of the Kremlin, Chisty Boulevard No. 12 was built in 1912 by Sergei Vashkov (1879-1914), the designer of churchware. In the middle two floors of the originally five-storey block (two storeys were added in 1945) are stunning highly stylised bas-reliefs of plants and animals (78) inspired by the unique 12th century sculpture that adorns the churches of Vladimir to the east of Moscow, an art form lost during the Mongol

78 Vashkov, Chisty Boulevard apartments, 1912: reliefs based on the carvings of the churches in Vladimir envelop the facade.

80 Bondarenko, Tokmakov Lane Church, 1907-08: the first Old Believer church in Moscow after the ban was lifted, its most striking feature is the unusual belfry with angel mosaics.

Our Lady – and, constructed in only one year from May 1907 to June 1908, was the first new Old Believer church in Moscow to be built after the signing of the decree on freedom of worship. It also functioned as an important social centre for the community. In 1930 it was shut and its congregation, swollen by influxes from other Old Believer churches closed earlier, were obliged to use the church at the Preobrazhenskoe monastery across the Yauza River. Today hidden behind tall apartment blocks (Nos 13/15) that screen it totally from the street, the church is greatly mutilated, its form truncated and deformed by the removal of its cupolas, by new windows cruelly cut into the walls or the enlargement of old ones, and by ugly additions that crudely flank the front porch. It has been used variously as a children's theatre, library, garment factory, and is now an engravers and stamp workshop making writing materials for schools. Yet more than enough remains of the church to spark the imagination.

Bondarenko borrowed from the architecture of the ancient churches of Novgorod and Pskov, their bare masonry cuboid walls and elaborate arched entranceways, the small windows and the roof *zvonnitsa* or belfry. Here on Tokmakov Lane the west entrance is dominated by a highly decorated archway jutting out from the building and contrasting with the plain brick walls that are interrupted only by a small triptych of a window. But the eye flies involuntarily upward to the odd belfry. It is shielded by a steeply pitched roof upheld by stubby columns and

wonderful ceramic tiles in the gable of two angels gracefully holding the icon of the church's dedication. Oddly, there is now a hole in the tiles where someone has removed the representation of the icon, perhaps afraid of its baletul influence on those who have desecrated the church.

In his reverence for traditional Russian architecture, Bondarenko was not averse to

using the latest technology and he was able to incorporate reinforced concrete for the long body of the church thus avoiding the usual supporting piers and creating a large unobstructed interior space capable of accommodating up to five hundred people. Since this was one of the priestless Old Believer sects, the religious services were conducted by elders and therefore took place before the iconostasis in full view of the

81 Shchusev, Church of the Intercession, 1908-12: borrowings from medieval Russian churches are effectively combined for the convent church founded by Grand Duchess Elizaveta Fyodorovna.

ancient prototypes in Novgorod. The tower, however, recalls the wooden octagonal churches of the north. But in the end the Church of the Intercession is utterly itself, a stylisation which has become something different and new, its contours and flowing lines expressing the plasticity and movement of Art Nouveau.

The tower was originally covered in gilded ceramic tiles as was the large helmet-shaped cupola making a brilliant feast of colour against the cream, stuccoed walls. Within, the icons placed around the walls and on the iconostasis and the furnishings were especially rich thanks to the generous gifts of Stepan Ryabushinsky from his unique collection (see chapter two). A charming gate and fencing in the medieval style originally surrounded it. When the church was closed the icons, including nine especially valuable ones of 15th century Novgorod from the important deisis row of the iconostasis, and all the elaborate churchware and chandeliers also designed in the Art Nouveau manner, were confiscated by the Tretyakov and other museums. The church was further debased when in 1966 it was given to the sports society 'Spartak' and Bondarenko's spacious interior was found to be ideal as a sports hall. In 1995 the dilapidated church was returned to the now much depleted Old Believer community. Soon crosses reappeared on the cupolas and repairs were painstakingly inaugurated. It is to be fervently hoped that the long postponed Third Automobile Ring road in Moscow, which would result in its destruction, will not now be built.

84 Shchusev, Church of the Intercession: an angel by Mikhail Nesterov is juxtaposed with an icon of the Virgin under restoration.

Two Orthodox Churches

Another outstanding Art Nouveau church is to be found in Zamoskvoreche, Moscow's attractive district which lies across the river from the Kremlin. Old Believer communities had also settled in this district and several churches were built for them in the 1900s, but none as outstanding as the Bondarenko churches in the east end. The Church of the Intercession of

OPPOSITE
83 Shchusev, Church of the Intercession: the main western entrance with a painting of Christ by Nesterov.

the Martha and Mary Convent or Sisters of Mercy is, however, not Old Believer but Orthodox, its style a personal choice of a high-ranking member of the royal family.

Grand Duchess's Church of the Intercession

The convent was founded by Grand Duchess Elizaveta Fyodorovna, a princess of Hesse-Darmstadt, granddaughter of Queen Victoria and sister of the Tsaritsa Alexandra, who had married the notorious Sergei Alexandrovich, uncle of the Tsar and Governor-General of Moscow. The unpopular Grand Duke in the troubled year 1905 was despatched by a terrorist's bomb at the Nikolsky Gate of the Kremlin as he was driving out in his carriage. A brutal man and notoriously homosexual, he had not been an ideal husband. His widow, perhaps thankfully, retired from the world, formed the Martha and Mary Community of Sisters of Mercy, and dedicated the rest of her life to good works. She built her open convent (most of the sisters had not taken their vows) about one kilometre south of the Kremlin and invited the well established young architect/restorer, Alexei Shchusev (1873-1949), to design the main church, 1908-12 (81), as the centre of the ensemble of hospital and residential buildings. Shchusev had made a name for himself as a talented restorer of ancient churches in Russia and just at the time he undertook the Grand Duchess's commission, he was appointed Academician for his reconstruction of the 12th century church of St Vasily at Ovruch in the Ukraine. Later he was to display a phenomenal ability to adapt to new political directions in architecture. The designer of Lenin's mausoleum, he went on to become the leading architect of the monumental Soviet classical style of the 1930s and 1940s.

The debt to the early churches of Pskov and Novgorod and Vladimir is obvious in Shchusev's building but the forms are so exaggerated and finely manipulated that it could never be confused with its archetypes. For one thing the Church of the Intercession is much larger than the medieval churches. Here the dominant form is the hugely heavy helmet-shaped cupola placed squarely at the centre of the cube. It is balanced at the eastern end by the vast triple apse, and on the west the greatly extended so-called refectory which is, unusually, the same width as the church. The church is entered from the western portal under the head of Christ by the artist, Mikhail Nesterov (1862-1942), who was an Abramtsevo habitué (83). Overhead onion domes, so slim they seem distorted, identify the two roof belfries like the *zvonnitsy* on 16th century churches. The plain walls are dotted with brick decoration; impressive limestone carvings by the sculptor, Sergei Konenkov (1874 - 1971), are placed over the porches and on the apse. The windows are the long narrow slits adopted in a northern country where heating was always a factor to be considered. Asymmetry is also a feature; the north and south portals are not the same size and the north alone is decorated with reliefs. Mikhail Nesterov painted the frescoes of the interior, the iconostasis with its delicate angels (84), and on the east wall of the refectory, the splendid painting *Toiling and Burdened Rus going to Meet Christ* and he even designed the grey nuns' habits. The heavy, monolithic gate to the street is also in keeping with the medieval spirit, the plain wall interrupted by an icon frame and large and small openings for carriages and pedestrians. A small fountain once played on the inner side of the wall.

The convent which included a small hospital, closed in 1918, and its church treasures were subsequently confiscated and lost. Elizaveta Fydorovna was arrested by the Bolsheviks in 1918 and died a horrific death along with other members of the royal family after being thrown down a well with explosives tossed in afterwards. The church became a cinema but eventually, after the Second World War, the state icon restoration workshop acquired it and managed to repair the damage inflicted during its time as a cinema. The workshop still occupies the building although the convent has been re-established and the sisters are demanding their church back. But somehow it is not inappropriate that this splendid church, itself an icon of Art Nouveau, should be the setting for the arduous, delicate repair of the huge great icons of the 15th and 16th centuries from northern Russia that crowd the spacious refectory.

Church of the Resurrection at Sokolniki

Just by the entrance to Sokolniki Park in north Moscow which in the early 1900s was at the extreme end of the city and heavily populated with dachas, another neo-Russian Orthodox church soars upward. The large Church of the Resurrection at Sokolniki built 1909-13 and designed by Pavel Tolstykh (1878-1939) is instantly recognisable as a reworking of the elegant architecture of the tall wooden tower churches of the north (85). It could also have been modelled on the tower church at Kolomenskoe, the forerunner to St Basils in Red Square, itself derived from the northern wooden towers. Unusually for an Orthodox church, the impetus for the new building came not from the conservative central church authorities but, like the Old Believer churches, from the local community, led by the archpriest, Father Ioann Kedrov. The stunningly beautiful church, funded by the local enthusiasts, enjoyed a singular degree of independence from the central authorities which may explain why the design is so unusually audacious for an Orthodox church of this time. It is unique among churches of this date too in that it was never closed or looted in the Soviet period, and has retained virtually all its original features, even those of the interior, the only Art Nouveau church to do so in Moscow.

Eight lesser cupolas are centrally grouped around the soaring octagonal tower, the main feature of the church, emphasising its upward thrust. The porch with its sharply gabled roof is set against a wall pierced by three long vertical windows which ends in scalloped overhanging eaves. The pale green of the walls contrasts forcefully with the broad white trim that

OPPOSITE
85 Tolstykh, Church
of the Resurrection,
1909-13: the tower
churches of the 16th
century and St Basils
in Red Square were
the inspiration for
this church.

accentuates each window, door and structural element of the building. No bell tower detracts from the symmetry of the resplendent building; instead it is cunningly incorporated into the church to the right of the entrance and its cupola is included in those surrounding the tower. Even the service buildings in the courtyard behind the church faithfully observe the same design as the main building. Unlike traditional Orthodox churches, there are no colourful frescoes covering every inch of the interior space but only a few striking oil paintings against tranquilly white walls. The Art Nouveau iconostasis is made of dark, almost black, pear and cypress wood carved in a basket-weave pattern that is repeated in the other church furniture – the panelling and icon frames – and forming a dark contrast to the white walls thus focusing the eye on the iconostasis. The original huge chandelier with the fashionable opaque shades of the period hangs from the inside of the dome At the express wish of Father Ioann, another unusual feature of the church was adopted; the apse faces south in the direction of Palestine rather than east. Father Ioann, who was arrested and died in a Soviet camp, was canonised in 1992.

The church has had an unusual and interesting history. Its first choir, which was composed exclusively of blind singers, was celebrated for the high quality of its music. With the advent of Soviet power, several attempts were made by the district and central authorities to have the church closed and turned into a club or vegetable warehouse or even demolished, but for one reason or another, these proved unsuccessful even when workers from the local factories joined in the campaign. One explanation as to why it escaped the fate suffered by most churches at this time was its occupation in the 1930s by the 'Renovationists', a reforming church movement under the control of the Bolsheviks which was later eliminated. In the 1930s, as the anti-religious campaign gathered momentum and church after church was closed or demolished, precious icons and other valuable objects were spirited away and brought to the Church of the Resurrection for safe-keeping. The famous icon of the Iberian virgin which stood in a chapel at the entrance to Red Square was brought here and given place of honour when the chapel and gates were destroyed (it is now rebuilt). Other important icons at the Kremlin and Kitai-gorod gates were also placed here for safety. When Stalin made his peace with the church during the Second World War, the council in 1945 at which the new patriarch, Alexei, was elected was held in this building. After that, until the restoration of the position of the church in the 1990s, many other important synodal meetings took place there. The lovely building, which makes such a colourful scene with Sokolniki Park in the background, is now hidden from view on two sides by ugly, unnecessary and thoughtless high-rise towers erected in 1979.

CHAPTER FOUR

WORLD OF COMMERCE

At the turn of the century the unprecedented expansion of the Russian economy and the equivalent growth in trade and commerce, particularly in Moscow, meant that a whole variety of new buildings were ugently required. Banks and insurance companies, trading groups, clubs, publishing houses and the ubiquitous factories. began to proliferate at an extraordinary rate. It should be mentioned that these institutions were scarcely known in old Moscow, where almost all economic activities were confined to the marketplace, and handmade goods and cottage industries provided most of the necessities of life. Their explosive appearance must have had a dramatic impact on a society only beginning to adjust to the end of serfdom. Although the new commercial buildings were put up rapidly, often in less than a year, their solid construction and fine craftsmanship have ensured that they have survived the turbulent 20th century uncommonly well. These buildings with some notable exceptions especially the new apartment blocks, reflected the practicalities of economics and business by their emphasis on rationality of construction and more prudent, less extravagant treatment. This was a more judicious and pragmatic interpretation of Art Nouveau.

With this furious growth, appeared a huge demand for residential housing as near to the centre of the city as possible. As individual houses took up too much land and were becoming more uneconomic, apartment blocks of several storeys began to make their appearance throughout the heart of Moscow from the 1890s onwards. five storeys, which once seemed shockingly high, were quickly superseded by taller buildings. Stanislavsky in *My Life in Art* relates how Chekhov in 1904 as he lay dying was still able to express delight on being told of the Alfremov apartment block then going up to an unprecedented eight storeys and how he 'strongly saw in it portents of future Russian and world culture...'. The new apartments intended for the wealthy, expanding bourgeoisie provided seven or more spacious rooms included servants quarters and back stairs for tradesmen. Housing for the poor, however, was left to the inadequately funded charities and the city government, most of whose members were the very factory owners who were stolidly indifferent to the plight of their employees. Although a surprising number of subsidised apartment blocks were eventually constructed from money bequeathed by conscience-stricken merchants at the end of their lives, even the low rents of these apartments proved too costly for most factory workers and, in any case, were insufficient in number to meet the demand of the huge influx of peasants from the countryside.

Moscow's population grew at the astonishing rate of sixty-five percent between 1862, the year after emancipation, and 1871, when the first proper census was taken. By the 1890s it had topped the one million mark and by 1912 it was over one and a half million. The rapid growth was not only due to immigration from the countryside but also to the higher birth rate which depended upon recent improvements in hygiene, especially the availability of clean water. Nevertheless, the poor continued to live in hovels or izbas or the overcrowded and loathesome factory barracks in the outer districts beyond the Garden Ring. Moscow remained a city of great contrasts between the very rich and the extremely poor, the educated and the illiterate, the mansion and the hovel.

APARTMENT BUILDING BOOM

Before the 1870s, Moscow was a rambling city full of empty plots of land and small wooden houses rarely more than two storeys high, each with its own garden. These small houses were counterbalanced by a great number of picturesque churches and the many classical mansions of the nobility with their large gardens. After 1870 the picture changed radically and not only with the appearance of new factories. The huge Cathedral of Christ the Saviour near the Kremlin profoundly altered the old city landscape and in the 1880s and 1890s the new museums, the city Duma and the great shopping arcade now known as GUM, transformed the central district around Red Square (see pp 16-21). Now the whole of central Moscow was to undergo a radical alteration in appearance.

By the end of the century, Moscow experienced a severe lack of adequate housing for persons in the middle income range; these included the managers of the new factories, those in the traditional professions, and the traders and clerks. Within the centre bounded by the Garden Ring road where the new bourgeois preferred to live, space was limited and there was no alternative but to construct as rapidly as possible good quality apartment blocks on the model of European cities like Paris or Brussels. The new construction companies would buy up old 18th century town estates in the centre of the city that had for a century or more occupied large lots, demolish them, and build new apartment blocks of five or even more storeys within the same boundaries. These were sold to the burgeoning middle and professional classes eager to obtain large and well appointed modern homes. It was a highly profitable business but, to their credit, or perhaps to attract well-heeled clients in the face of fierce competition, the building firms did not stint on the quality of the construction or the services provided, and called upon the most proficient and best known architects to design their buildings.

The advent of the electric tram in 1904 helped to extend the area of easy access to the city centre and, accordingly, apartment blocks were built in an ever widening arc from the Kremlin outwards. The great growth in apartment housing in Moscow coincided with the reign of Art Nouveau and it is true to say that the surge of new housing is closely bound up with, indeed greatly facilitated the dominance of the new style. In particular, the innovations in technology and construction methods combined with the freer use of space provided by Art Nouveau, greatly enhanced the modern apartment block. These buildings were solidly built, utilising the latest technology to obtain a structure firmly

86 Kekushev, Isakov apartments, 1904-06: fine railings of the central staircase.

supported by reinforced concrete and iron struts. On the whole, even those apartment houses with the most original designs were conservative in the sense that the interior had to be comfortable and attractive to a rather conservative clientele, and the style of the exterior, whimsical as it might be, could not be continued within except in the entrance hall and main staircase. The principal interest of the builder was, after all, in making a large profit and he had to keep the clients' interests firmly in mind when indulging the imagination of his architect. He succeeded amazingly well in constructing good quality housing for, even with virtually no maintenance, Muscovites have continued to live in them for nearly a century in disgracefully over-crowded conditions never envisaged by the architects. Yet not only are they still standing but many are supporting extra floors added in the 1930s.

Isakov Apartments

Lev Kekushev's apartment house for the Trading/ Construction Company is one of the master-pieces of Art Nouveau in Moscow. Built between 1904 and 1906 on Prechistenka Street, No. 28, a handsome street in the heart of the aristocratic district, it was sold on completion to the Petersburg merchant, Ivan Pavlovich Isakov, by whose name it is usually known. The five-storey building flush with the street is all flowing movement as the eye follows the line of the protruding second- to fourth-storey end bays and central recessed alcove sculpted out of the brickwork. Indeed, there seems to be a palpable tension between the lushness of the facade and the overall symmetry of the building. The plain dark stone ground floor is offset by the light green glazed brick and flesh-pink stone trim of the three central storeys punctuated by lion masks and ladies' heads. Delicate wrought-iron balconies with a striking circular design, repeated on the staircase within (86), are set into the central recessed bay. The upper floor is decorated by a fine abstract floral pattern that flows like a frieze in and around the pediment where two female figures represent enlightenment, one bearing a torch, the other a book (87). A deeply overhanging metal cornice curves and flows, throwing its shadow over the two ladies. From the street beneath looking up one has the impression of a patterned hat with a wide brim crowning the building.

The H-shape of the block allows for two different sections; the apartments on the street

87 Isakov apartments: two ladies representing enlightenment adorn the pediment protected by the metal overhanging curved cornice.

side are large, of seven or eight rooms, with only two flats on each floor and servants stairs near the kitchens. The back or courtyard side of the H is divided into six floors, and has smaller apartments. For long in use as communal housing after 1917, one family to a room, the original large apartments are now being restored and the Isakov house is once again commercially viable. One hopes the trend to turn all available accomodation into commercial offices will not apply in this case and that it will remain, as it was intended to be, a building of commodious and comfortable apartments.

DUBOVSKY'S OPULENT BUILDINGS
Ostozhenka Apartments

Not far away, at the beginning of Ostozhenka, the parallel street to Prechistenka, on a corner plot, another exceptional apartment building was constructed 1907-08. The architect, Valentin Dubovsky (1877-1931), became known as a builder of particularly luxurious apartment buildings. Born in Petersburg and brought up by his artist uncle, he was early attracted to painting and then studied architecture at the Institute of Civil Engineers. Like so many other budding architects, he was drawn to Moscow by the opportunities afforded in the frenzy of new construction. For a time he designed stations for the Yaroslavl railway line, but he soon moved to the field of housing and is responsible for the construction of fifteen apartment blocks in Moscow from 1906 to 1915. After the revolution he took part in the planning of the new electric power stations set up by Lenin, including the huge one at Shatura, southeast of Moscow.

The ornate apartment building for the businessman/merchant Yakov Mikhailovich Filatov was Dubovsky's earliest building in Moscow that has survived and is the one most redolent of Art Nouveau (88). The five-sectioned block of five to six floors was so near the gigantic Cathedral of Christ the Saviour, that the architect decided to emphasise the fact. On the courtyard side of the building facing the cathedral which would normally have been left plain, he devised an interesting cornice that projects above the roof line as if greeting the cathedral. On the main facades, Dubovsky's skills were employed to the full especially on the one facing narrow Obydensky Lane. Crowning the corner with an octagonal cone like a wooden church, he continued the fantasy on the bays facing the lane using coloured tiles and sculpted ornament. The spindly stems of weird, other-worldly plants ascend almost the full height of the building to erupt in strange flowers so grotesque they give the appearance of an octopus. The design continues to evolve into shells and other strange forms that resemble an alarming face glaring down on the passerby. Tall hooded cornices and

strange, moulded roofs add to the impression of a fantasy world (89). Indeed, looking at this building one might think one was in Barcelona with Gaudi rather than Moscow. The original doors and staircase survive in the spacious entrance hall that, although now shabby and decayed, still recall a former grandeur. When the apartment block was completed the influential *Moscow Weekly* angrily declared: 'Every New Year brings Moscow several dozen new monstrously ugly buildings, which tear into the city streets with that special boldness characteristic of Moscow. Where else would one find anything like the new building [by Dubovsky] at the beginning of Ostozhenka'.

Castle on the Arbat

Dubovsky built a second apartment house for the same entrepreneurial Filatov family in 1913-14 on the eve of the First World War (90). It was located on the Arbat, one of the most ancient roads in Moscow and a fashionable address before the revolution when most of its inhabitants belonged to the nobility or were merchants of the first guild. After 1917 they were replaced as tenants of the splendid turn of the century apartment blocks by members of the Moscow intelligentsia, living like everyone else in one room per family. These *Children of the Arbat* whose life is chronicled in Anatoly Rybakov's novel, would have witnessed in the Stalin years the weekly episode of police terror when the Arbat was arbitrarily closed as Stalin, departing from the Kremlin on the way to his

88 Dubovsky, Ostozhenka apartments, 1908: the eerie decor of these opulent apartments is based on plants that slither up the wall to erupt in strange flowerings.

dacha, swept past in his menacing cavalcade of black limousines. In the mid-1980s the Arbat lost its prestige and its atmosphere when, in the name of restoration, it was tarted up in a theatrical fashion and turned into a pedestrian street full of stalls and cheap amusements.

Dubovsky, assisted by Nikolai Arkhipov (1895-1959), created his most extravagant building here. Built around the theme of a medieval castle, it was to be the largest on the Arbat and still is if the high-rise 'wedding palace' used by the Ministry of Foreign Affairs at the end is not counted. Rising up through eight storeys the substantially modified Art Nouveau

forms are noticeable in the pointed pediments and in the rythmic ebb and flow of seven bays, squared instead of rounded, some of which break through the roof as crenellated towers. Two medieval knights in full armour stand on guard in niches on the main corner tower. It is the ultimate in whimsical facades. For many years now the luxurious apartments have served as offices for the Russian Ministry of Culture.

Prince Makaev's Building

Apartment construction was also taking place at a feverish pace in eastern Moscow between the Boulevard and the Garden Ring. Among several

interesting buildings on Podsosensky Lane erected in the early 1900s, the striking apartment house of 1903 by the Georgian prince, Georgy Makaev (1871- after 1917), exemplifies Art Nouveau at its most curvilinear and engaging (91). Taking full advantage of the corner site, the architect manipulates plant motifs and horizontal banding to invigorate the facade of this extravagant building. At the dramatic corner elevation the two facades meet, one with protruding wrought iron balconies, the other by contrast round and sculptured. The corner bay itself seems to flow out of the ground floor rising through the long thin stems of two tulips ending in blue coloured tiles and a medieval lookout tower which soars above the main building. The assymetrically placed windows are finely dressed in Art Nouveau designs, their forms underlined by stone architraves and horizontal linking bands at the ground floor level which contrast with the roughcast plasterwork. The best of the windows, on Podsosensky Lane (93), provides a bed out of which stylised flowers climb the wall to the top floor. A tremendously exhilarating building which provides a lively contrast with a classical building on the opposite corner. Prince Makayev was an active member of the charity that provided housing for the poor and was also a director of the firm K. Ermans & Co (see p. 122).

Sokol (Falcon) Building

In central Moscow on Kuznetsky Most, the main shopping street, Ivan Mashkov (1867-1945), of the Moscow Architectural Society (editor of the

excellent 1915 Moscow guide book), built the five-storey Sokol (Falcon) building, 1902-03, on a narrow, awkward site (94). Of five storeys, the first two with large plate-glass windows were intended for commercial purposes while the three upper storeys were set aside for apartments. Paired windows and round bays provide a play of curves and planes and blue tiles discreetly positioned between the bands of windows give

90 Dubovsky and Arkhipov, Castle on the Arbat, 1913-14: the medieval knight stands guard over one of Moscow's most luxurious apartment buildings.

OPPOSITE
89 Ostozhenka apartments: detail of one of the bays showing the moulded roofs and weird designs.

91 Prince Makaev s building, 1903: horizontal banding and plant motifs dominate especially the corner tower with its slim tulips ending in a band of blue tiles.

colour and contrast with the cream stucco. The principle point of interest however is above where the central bay with its two scooped out balconies and elegant metal fencing supports a ceramic triple-sectioned pediment portraying a falcon soaring in the bright blue sky over the wavy sea. It is by Nikolai Sapunov (1880-1912), a promising theatre designer whose career came to an untimely end when he drowned at the age of thirty-two. The panel, a splendid reminder in the narrow confines of the old city of the far-off seas bordering Russia, echoes the dramatic ceramic panels on the pediments of the nearby Metropole Hotel. The Sokol building is now used not inappropriately for the offices of various airlines.

Stroganov School Apartments
Between 1904 and 1907 on busy Myasnitskaya (Butcher) Street which connects the main Post Office to the square of the three main railway stations, Fyodor Shekhtel constructed a large apartment building (92) as a commercial development for the enterprising Stroganov School of Technical Design. The school, at that time located only a few streets away on Rozhdestvenka, was founded in 1825 by the far-sighted archaeologist, Count Sergei Grigorievich Stroganov (1794-1882), in order to encourage good design in the crafts and nascent commercial arts. By the early 1900s its reputation was such that it attracted outstanding avant-garde artists like Rodchenko and Stepanova. After the revolution, it was merged with the School of Art,

Sculpture and Architecture to form the experimental and liberal art schools of the 1920s, Vkhutemas and Vkhutein. In 1945 it again became a separate institution.

The building, its restrained design so unlike the extravagance of Shekhtel's mansions, takes up an entire block fronting onto Myasnitskaya and the two lanes, Bankovsky and Krivokolenny. It can be imagined as the letter E, where the middle of the letter extends into the garden of the courtyard. The ground and first floors of reinforced concrete with their huge plate-glass windows and niches above for advertising typography, provided excellent premises for commercial enterprises and reflected

the growing practice in Moscow by which the old system of arcades was being replaced by shops along the main streets. The top three floors were for apartments which, although not as luxurious as other new blocks in Moscow, were spacious (each with four to seven rooms). The complex included many unusual amenities for the time such as its own central heating system, an electricity generator, a laundry, basement storage rooms and, most unusually in Moscow, garages for the increasing number of automobile owners.

The apartment block has survived uncommonly well and still if only faintly exhibits subdued, highly refined, Art Nouveau traits. The

92 Shekhtel, Stroganov apartments, 1904-07: unlike Shekhtel s earlier buildings the apartments are restrained and not showy, the fine delicate ceramic panels virtually the only ornament.

93 Prince Makaevs building, 1903:
the principal window firmly etched with
flowers and vertical lines that continue
upward to the top of the building.

94 Mashkov, Sokol (Falcon) building, 1902-03:
the round bay with audacious ironwork gives way
to the large ceramic panel of a falcon (by Nicolai
Sapunov) soaring over white-capped waves.

Ermans Perfume Factory

Moscow became a leading centre in Russia for the production of scent at the turn of the century, when it was largely in the hands of foreigners. The German, K. L. Ermans, (Ehrmanns) began manufacturing pharmaceuticals, chemicals and perfumery in 1889 which achieved an annual turnover in the 1900s of over one million rubles. In 1907 the architect, Vasily Yeramishantsev (1875-1958), built him a splendid factory (99) on Vorontsovskaya Street, No. 10, near Taganka Square, a popular area for factories at that time. It is a supremely handsome building which extends for some length along the street; the slim red brick piers, sometimes flat sometimes hexagonal, contrasting with the white stucco of the windows especially the moulded recessed windows on the upper, third floor. Together with the round turrets at third floor level, they give it a vertical thrust ending at the large pointed pediment that completes the central protruding bay. The windows are large and in the central section triple-bayed which would have provided excellent lighting to the factory floor. Even the water tower poking up behind is an elegant structure, like a folded bud.

Three Remarkable Houses

The owners of the new factories, only one or two generations removed from the peasantry, liked to have their homes close to their place of work, in many cases right against the walls within the territory of the factory. In north Moscow at Krasnoselskoe near the square of the three railway stations, Alexei Abrikosov, second generation peasant, founded in the 1880s a profitable confectionary business. His heirs who continued to own the confectionary, were outstanding in the fields of science, diplomacy and medicine. One daughter married the Czech liberal nationalist, Karel Kramar and another, Anna, adopted the Roman Catholic faith, a most unusual step in Orthodox Moscow. With her husband she established a centre for catholicism in Moscow suffering arrest and long imprisonment after the Bolsheviks took power. It was for this unusual family that the architect Boris Shnaubert (c.1860 - after 1917) built in 1902 a colourful two-storey red and white house next to their factory (100). The corner mansion exhibits strongly moulded windows and a spectacular triple bayed section over the entrance that culminates in a round pediment and stylised ironwork at roof level. It is here that Anna Abrikosova held her salon for fellow catholics. The confectionary continues to operate although under its post-revolution name of P. A. Babaev, a local Bolshevik.

The unusual neo-Russian house for the Bromley Brothers machine manufacturing factory, now Krasniye Proletarii (Red Workers), on Malaya Kaluzhskaya is in a similarly extravagant vein (101). It was built in 1911, rather late for Art Nouveau, by the architect Nikolai Butusov (1864 - after 1917) and displays a stylised porch and balcony standing on truncated green and red barley-twist columns, pointed window frames and sharp gables, highly distorted borrowings

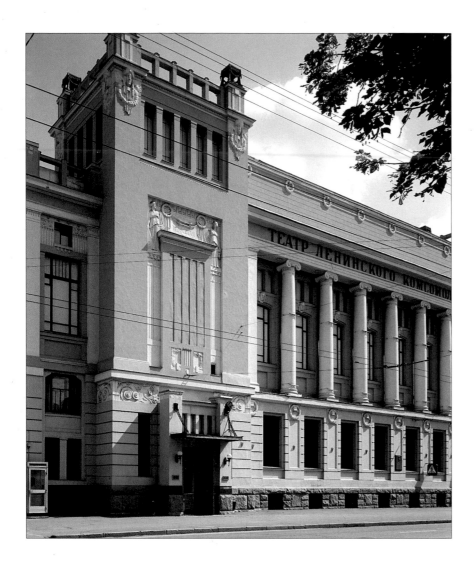

103 Ivanov-Shits, Merchants Club, 1907-08: the classical neo-Empire facade with giant Ionic columns belies the rich Art Nouveau treatment of the interior.

OPPOSITE
104 Merchants Club: unlike the neo-classical exterior, the interior is in a linear version of Art Nouveau like this hallway with its design in paint, stone and metal.

the building. The dark, dauntingly impressive rooms in green and copper give off an aura of that ponderous comfort associated with the portly bearded merchants. The wall and ceiling designs of squares, rectangles and straight lines, of angled rays meeting at pearl-coloured eye-like stones, and of female heads holding wreaths like those on the exterior facade, are executed in paint and metal and wood. The floors of composite stone beautifully echo the designs on the walls. The association with ancient Egypt

is especially strong in the dark wooden and stone architraves of the doors which recall the mysterious entrances to Egyptian tombs. Although some details have been lost, the club has on the whole survived well even to the extent that the original brass door handles are still in place and some of the original furniture, the cupboards and settees designed by Ivanov-Shits, still decorate the principle room, now the director's office.

The merchants were unceremoniously evicted in January, 1918, by anarchists who forcefully occupied the club for use as their headquarters two months before Lenin moved his new government to Moscow. The conservative merchants, already horribly shocked by the success of the Bolsheviks, must have been very disturbed by the antics of the anarchists in their luxurious club. The anarchists remained in occupation for four months, turning the place upside down, hanging black flags out the windows, and generally causing an uproar. Originally allies of the Bolsheviks, they quickly fell out with them and by the spring of 1918 the Bolshevik secret police, the Cheka, was empowered to ruthlessly expel them from the club. The building was then expropriated as a communist party school, then a cinema and finally in 1933 for the experimental Theatre of Working Youth (TRAM). This free theatre was in its turn strangled as Stalin put pressure on all the arts to conform. Renamed the Lenin Komsomol after the communist party youth movement, the theatre came into its own during

OPPOSITE
107 Shekhtel, *Utro Rossii* printing house, 1907: set within a frame, the two glazed bays rise uninterrupted through three floors in this fine building for the merchants newspaper.

so rapidly that the printworks could hardly keep up with the demand. Several remarkable premises were constructed in the old city to accomodate the new publishing houses whose progressive nature was reflected in the avant-garde architecture of their buildings. It is not surprising that these new entrepreneurs, some only recently of the peasant class, chose the most imaginative of the architects to design their premises.

Levenson Printing House

Fyodor Shekhtel's first printing house was for Alexander Levenson, for whom he also constructed a uniqe dacha in Peredelkino in neo-Russian style. It was completed in 1900 within the Garden Ring on a lane parallel to Moscow's most central street, Tverskaya (Gorky) (105). The section facing the street, busy with sculpted forms, is for the offices of the firm while the printing house stretches deep into the territory behind. The initial impression is of a French chateau with the pointed corner towers, steep roofs and stucco parading as stonework but the building is merely a play on this theme. There is a fine relief on the third floor of a printer at his press watched by his assistant, illustrating the respect for crafts so vividly expressed at Abramtsevo and popularised in Russia through the works of William Morris. The relief, considered politically correct by the communist party, remained undefaced and the building continued to be used as a printing press in the Soviet period (the editorial offices have

recently become a bank). Protruding bays and corner towers exhibit one of the architect's favourite themes, a stylised thistle. The brick-work contrasts with the sculptural effect of the rendering, windows and doors are curved and bent, and there is delightfully delicate metalwork on the roof . The flowing wave-like interior staircase duplicates that of Shekhtel's Ryabushinsky House begun in the same year. But the building is also practical, the frame construction allows for the large windows so necessary in the work of the printers. The press was built very quickly, in less than a year and impatiently occupied before it was even finished.

Sytin's Newspaper on Tverskaya

Ivan Sytin (1851-1934) came to Moscow as an uneducated village boy where he found work on the street selling books. Eventually, through great energy and perseverance he was able to take over the stalls and then to start his own publishing house. He joined Tolstoy's circle and through its influence became an enthusiast for the expansion of education in Russia. To this end he published encyclopedias, books and magazines for children, and extremely cheap pocket editions of the classics. He was one of the first to publish contemporary Russian writers like Chekhov and Tolstoy and Gorky with all of whom he was on close terms. In the Soviet period, too, his success continued for he was much admired as a publisher of books for the masses and was employed as a consultant for his own now nationalised publishing firm. Although one of

the despised bourgeois, he was even granted a state pension in 1928 when he retired. Furthermore, unlike nearly everyone else of middle class in Moscow, he was not expelled from his home after the revolution but allowed to continue to live in the grand fourth and fifth floor penthouse apartment created especially for him and his family when the newspaper building was constructed.

Adolf Erikhson (1862 - after 1917), a graduate of the Moscow School of Painting, Sculpture and Architecture, and then in his forties, was by that time a successful Moscow architect of mansions and commercial buildings. For Sytin he built the Russkoe Slovo newspaper building on Tverskaya (Gorky) Street just north of Strastnoi (Pushkin) Square, 1905 - 07, using the walls and foundations of an existing early 19th century Moscow house (106). Strictly symmetrical, of three, four and five tall floors it bears the hallmarks of early Art Nouveau with its light glazed brick, curved mullions, different sized windows and interesting stepped roofline. A frieze of tiles depicting brightly coloured flowers brightens the space between the second and third floors which were used as the editorial offices of the newspaper. In the penthouse apartment on the fourth and fifth (attic) floors are large round windows the height of the floors. Erikhson's concrete and metal frame allowed for large windows and unhindered open spaces for the printing works. It is a vigorous and pleasant design for a building which was clearly intended to draw attention to itself.

Russkoe Slovo (Russian Word) was a liberal newspaper which by 1917 had a circulation of over one million, the largest in Moscow. It was published here until July 1918 when it was finally closed and the building was taken over for the main Bolshevik newspapers, Pravda and Izvestiya. In 1979 the Sytin publishing house, as happened to other buildings in the late 1930s on Tverskaya Street, was successfully moved thirty-four yards north to make room for the construction of the new building of *Izvestiya* next door.

Sytin's Publishing House on Pyatnitskaya

The main printing press of Sytin's expanding empire was located in Zamoskvoreche on the south side of old Moscow on Pyatnitskaya Street. Sytin had purchased the property in the 1880s and established his press there. In 1905 Adolf Erikhson, already engaged on the Tverskaya newspaper press, constructed the new five-storey building. But printers with their access to publications and power to halt the presses were traditionally in the forefront of labour unrest. The year of 1905 that began with Bloody Sunday, the shooting of up to a hundred peacefully protesting people in Petersburg by Tsarist troops, continued to be plagued with strikes and armed clashes. In the Zamoskvoreche district, Sytin's workers were heavily involved in these troubles. In January, 1,200 went on strike and dispersed to persuade other printworks to do the same. In August they demanded a reduction in the working day and improvements in pay, which Sytin rejected. In September they renewed their strike, followed by other sympathetic printers until by the end of the month no newspapers were published in Moscow. Unappeased by the Tsar's manifesto of 19 October promising to establish a parliament, the printers increased their opposition. On 7 December they were again on strike and Marxist cells in their organisation illegally published on the Sytin presses the first issue of *Izvestiya*. A huge demonstration of workers from other factories in Zamoskvoreche spontaneously gathered in front of the Sytin building on 10 December and the following day barricades were thrown up around the building. Tsarist troops attacked and broke through the barricades and that night set fire to the building. The fire engines which arrived to quell the flames were prevented from approaching and the recently completed edifice soon burnt to the ground forcing the Marxist printers within to withdraw.

Sytin commissioned Erikhson, to reconstruct the printing house which survived well although somewhat altered in 1912 by Ivan German (1875-late 1920s). The building has as its central axis two broad corner bays, while the more modern accomodation blocks for the printing works fan out from them in long, horizontal bands on both streets. Of five tall storeys, the corner is defined by vertical brick piers which contrast with the rendered infill of the windows and which rise three floors high. At the fifth floor they flow gently into corbels that support the narrow towers of square gables. The brick line swoops

down on either side almost to the next floor, overlapping the windows behind which peep out timidly resembling the resolution of the upper part of Erikhson's other printing house for Sytin on Tverskaya.

'Utro Rossii' Printing House

In 1907 Fyodor Shekhtel elaborated on the frame design with maximum glazing for yet another building for the Ryabushinsky family, the printing works of their newspaper, *Utro Rossii* (Morning of Russia) (107). The paper was the

108 Shekhtel, Ryabushinsky bank, 1903-04: rational but aesthetic with rounded corners and delicate ornament at the upper level it suits the serious business of banking.

109 Meisner, Ponizovsky building, 1901: the wrought-iron gates in the whiplash design are frequently encountered in Moscow.

BANKS AND OFFICES OF MOSCOW'S 'CITY'

The financial institutions of Moscow grew and expanded in line with the increase in industrial production and the escalation in trade and commerce for which Moscow had become the most important centre in Russia. As the merchant classes moved into the banks and finance houses they brought with them their architects, already tested in the construction of individual houses and industrial buildings, and unleashed them on Kitai-gorod, the Russian version of the City in London. This part of old Moscow, bounded by the Moskva River on the south, Red Square on the west, and by the thick walls of Kitaigorod on the north and east, was rapidly being built up with sober financial institutions. Although Art Nouveau was still in vogue it was applied for the banks and trading houses in a less flamboyant manner than that indulged in for private mansions or extravagant railway stations eager to attract passengers. These conservative institutions required a more sober and prudent treatment in order to reflect the seriousness and solidity which in those days characterised the world of money. Nevertheless, the quirky nature of Art Nouveau still occasionally shows through (109); other examples include three buildings designed by the foremost Moscow architect, Fyodor Shekhtel.

Arshinov Building

In 1899 Shekhtel completed for his client, Vasily Arshinov, an office and trading building for

mouthpiece for some of the merchants who, although not radicals in the political sense, were critical of the Tsar's government and lobbied for a more progressive economic policy and fewer restraints on capitalist development. Here the two recessed glazing bays supported by iron beams are almost uninterrupted for three floors until they resolve themselves in delicately rounded arches. The attic floor was more lively originally when, unpierced by windows, it displayed the typography announcing the name of the newspaper. The corners of the building are rounded, almost its only decorative device apart from the typography at the top and the contrast between materials – the brown glazed brick and the cream stonework of the lintels and string course. This admirable, powerful building is still in use as a printing works.

various goods especially cloth in the heart of Kitai-gorod that could be termed the first commercial building in Art Nouveau style in Moscow. It is composed of a dramatic giant arch extending up through the three floors used for the display and warehousing of goods. The arch takes up most of the street facade and is balanced by the smaller narrow windows ranged along the fourth, top floor like a cornice where the offices were situated (110). A brilliant contrast is provided by the cream stone windows set against the turquoise glazed brick, an unusual colour, but this is softened by the scrolling of the elaborate medallions and ladies heads as in a baroque building. The striving for maximum light and minimum structural elements in the use of thinner floors and the employment of lettering (now gone) to advertise the wares, an innovation just beginning to be accepted, place it squarely in the ranks of modern buildings.

110 Shekhtel, Arshinov building, 1899: the first Art Nouveau commercial building in Moscow, the giant arch rises three storeys and is brilliantly coloured, cream against turquoise.

Ryabushinsky Bank

A few years after the Arshinov building was completed around the corner from it on Birzheva (stock exchange) Square, Fyodor Shekhtel constructed in 1903-04 another building for Moscow's business community, the main bank of the influential Ryabushinsky Brothers (108). This is the first building in which functionalism and the aesthetic vied for first place. Originally arranged on five floors, four of framed triple-bay glazing for the spacious banking halls within and the fifth expressed in rhythmic narrow windows for the bank offices, it is a pared down version of the Arshinov Company building, lacking its dramatic colours and heavy curved ornament, but sharing its frame construction and attention to glazing. It is a clearer, more subdued, building expressed in serene cream and white, which nevertheless is softened by rounded corners and a minimal amount of ornament in the charming sea urchins or stylised dragons of the medallions. It was altered in 1913 when Alexander Kuznetsov, the pioneer in Moscow of reinforced concrete, added the top, sixth floor spoiling the original arrangement. The building suffered further when the typically Soviet porch was added and the entrance was moved from right to centre. It now houses the offices of the Russian Ministry of Labour.

Moscow Merchants' Society

The third and best in Shekhtel's trilogy of sober office buildings is the headquarters for the Moscow Merchants' Society also situated in Kitai-gorod and built 1909-10. It was to be Shekhtel's last commercial building and it is certainly one of his finest. It takes up almost a whole block and faces three streets of which the main one is Novaya Ploshchad just within the old Kitai-gorod wall (demolished in the 1930s). Plate-glass windows providing ceiling to floor glazing set within a narrow skeleton of reinforced concrete result in an overall mathematical grid which is simply breathtaking in this most modern of Shekhtel's buildings (111). Again it is a frame-work, built up in a series of deeply inset glazed bays divided by vertical piers in the already familiar pattern but here the windows extend into the attic floor and end only at the over-hanging flat roof originally built of reinforced concrete. The names of the different merchant companies were placed on the sections dividing the floors but have long since been obliterated. The unmistakable Art Nouveau character derives from the sensually curved piers, the recessed bays which softly ripple in repetitive rows, the contrast between the glazed brick and rendering of the windows, the ladies' masks of the top floor and the great moulded arch that leads into the courtyard on Novaya Ploshchad.

In 1918 immediately after the revolution it became the headquarters of the Bolshevik Commissariat for Health of the RSFSR, which had as its task the establishment of the new national health service under doctor Nikolai Semashko. It is now reverting to its original use as new businesses, formed after the fall of the

Soviet Union, vie for office space in Moscow.

The progression of Moscow architecture from the flamboyant early period of Art Nouveau as expressed in the mansions of Shekhtel and Kekushev to the sobriety and serenity of commercial buildings culminating in the Merchants' Society anticipates the arrival of constructivism in the 1920s where function was to be the overriding factor in design and

geometric forms were considered the ultimate in beauty. Before that happened, however, Art Nouveau suddenly came to an end not in some new natural development of its pioneering design and use of technology, but in the abrupt reappearance of the old-fashioned style most closely associated with the aristocracy of the late 18th and first half of the 19th century, the neo-classical.

111 Shekhtel, Moscow Merchants Society, 1909-10: a mathematical grid of large plate-glass windows set within a frame of reinforced concrete divided by rounded piers.

CHAPTER FIVE

DEMISE OF ART NOUVEAU AND THE TRIUMPH OF CLASSICISM

Art Nouveau in Moscow as everywhere else in Europe lasted not more than a decade. It was already well established when in 1904 the disastrous war against Japan broke out followed in 1905 by the stormy events of the first revolution which convulsed the country for nearly a year. Nicholas's promises of reform lapsed almost immediately the danger was over and the newly instituted parliament (Duma) was soon marginalised. A period of political conservatism and growing nationalism ensued, offset only by the attempted economic reforms of the Prime Minister, Petr Stolypin, which were already running into the sand when Stolypin was assassinated in 1911. Nicholas, meanwhile, having jealously guarded the role of supreme autocrat, was content to bury himself in petty details of government while ignoring the profound conflicts and contradictions afflicting the Tsarist regime. He was at the same time distracted by the illness of his son and heir, Alexei, who suffered from and fell increasingly under the influence of the reactionary and dissolute seer, Rasputin, who seemed able to alleviate the Tsarevich's symptoms. Thus Russia, deeply humiliated at the hands of the Japanese in 1904, and having turned its back on the opportunity for reform in 1905, was already in profound political crisis as it found itself helplessly caught up in Europe's drift towards the first World War. This troubled and reactionary political mood inevitably found expression in Russian society and, consequently, the arts, including architecture.

The reappearance of classical architecture thus coincided with, indeed reflected, the reaction against increasing instability and dissent in political and social life. It expressed in solid, three-dimensional form the essential inability of Russia, in spite of its undoubted industrial and commercial successes, to move ahead politically and socially. It also served as an expression of Russian nationalism for the preferred variant was the highly individual Empire style which had characterised Moscow in the early 19th century. A renewal of familiar Empire forms brought with it a nostalgia for the heroic era of the struggle against Napoleon and the illusory stability of old Russia after the French had been defeated. The noble architecture of columns and domes also recalled the romantic Golden Age of poetry and its two towering geniuses, Pushkin and Lermontov, the gentlemen poets who had both been exiled for their courageous stances.

DEATH OF ART NOUVEAU
The brilliance and wit of Art Nouveau with its disavowal of past styles, its daring use of new technology and materials, its search for new expressions of volume and form, was occasioned by staunch confidence in society and the future. As novelty was its hallmark, it could not have continued unabated for long and was bound to burn itself out. From its inception it had been bombarded by criticism from established architectural critics especially the conservative St Petersburgers where the new style had never completely taken hold. In the liberal and defiant

atmosphere of Moscow, Art Nouveau was more firmly rooted and the readoption of the classical style seemed more of a retrograde step.

The essence of Art Nouveau, its supreme individuality, had been a quality its early patrons, the up and coming merchants, had been anxious to express. But by the 1910s, these merchant dynasties had to a large extent not only been absorbed into Moscow society but they had risen to become its leading members in city government, in the economy and in the arts where they were important patrons. No longer were they excluded from holding titles and many accepted styles formerly the prerogative of the nobility. Nor did the nobility find it unseemly to mix and intermarry with people like the sugar-baron Kharitonenkos who were on close terms with such luminaries as Prince Shcherbatov and whose daughter married the highly placed Prince Gorchakov. They also found themselves more figureheads than managers in the running of their companies, when their role was replaced by boards and governors. So gradually, the singularity of the great merchants was eroded. Their taste for architecture likewise became less individual and more conventional and increasingly reflected that of the old establishment.

Strangely, it was the self-same architects of Art Nouveau who turned full circle to become the leaders of the classic revival. This was a phenomenon not only in Russia but in other European countries where architects of the calibre of Joseph Olbrich, Josef Hoffmann and Victor Horta were also weaned away from Art Nouveau and engaged in classicism albeit of a more stringent form. The English architect, R. Norman Shaw, had likewise turned from the Arts and Crafts movement to adopt a modified form of classicism.

In Russia a similar development occurred not only in architecture but in other branches of the arts: in music where Prokofiev and Stravinsky were rediscovering classical forms and in poetry where the Symbolists were being superseded by the classical Acmeists of whom Mandelshtam and Akhmatova were the most prominent. Architecture simply reflected the general trend of the times, of a regime and a society which preferred to look back and indulge in the nostalgia of the centenary of Napoleon's invasion of Russia in 1912 and a year later, in 1913, in the much vaunted tercentenary of the founding of the Romanov dynasty.

NEO-EMPIRE MANSIONS

In Moscow the model for the revival of classical architecture was not the austere 18th century mansions but that which was closer to hand, the late classical or Empire style in which the city was largely rebuilt after the devestating fire in 1812 of the French occupation. These were smaller, more comfortable houses or *osobnyaki*, usually of ochre colour and pleasingly decorated with mouldings and Ionic columns, bays and porches. In the Moscow of 1910, it was these attractive houses that inspired the designs for the elegant mansions of the next generation of the merchant class, who a decade earlier would have

112 Kuznetsov, Girls Grammar School, Bogorodsk (Noginsk), near Moscow, 1908: a masterful building for the Morozov textile clan by the pioneer of concrete and of factory architecture.

insisted on idiosyncratic Art Nouveau. Moscow's colourful variety which so distinguishes it from its great rival to the north, was not to be negated by tedious repetition of the same style; ochre two-storey neo-Empire mansions with their columns and mouldings stood next to floridly decorated asymmetrical Art Nouveau houses or medieval onion-domed churches. That is not to say these neo-Empire houses were indistinguishable from their predecessors – they differ in size, they are indifferent to the strict rules of symmetry and perhaps their most distinguishing feature is their free flowing arrangement of interior space. Of the examples that follow two were built as homes for leading Art Nouveau architects and three are now foreign embassies.

Alexander Kuznetsov's House

The fashion for the Empire style was so in vogue that even Alexander Kuznetsov (1875-1954), whose Art Nouveau buildings embellish the nearby textile town of Bogorodsk (112), and who pioneered the use of concrete in Moscow, chose in 1915 to rebuild an existing Empire house as his home rather than design a new one. Perhaps he preferred the privacy afforded by the enclosed enclave of the small estate located in the Prechistenka area. He retained the old facade complete with its five windows and pediment on Mansurov Lane but reworked the mouldings, rebuilt the entrance from the courtyard, redesigned the service buildings, and completely made over the interior in the freer manner of his Art Nouveau buildings.

Lazarev Mansion

Other architects adapted the Empire style to new mansions employing the lessons they had learned from Art Nouveau. On the same plot of land on Mertvy (Prechistensky) Lane, redeveloped by the Trading and Construction Company in the early 1900s, where William Walcot's two Art Nouveau villas stand, a third house was built in 1906 at the corner with Starokonyushenniy Lane (113). It is by Nikita Lazarev, who also designed an agreeable Art Nouveau apartment house not far away on the Arbat (114). It was purchased by Nikolai Mindovsky, director of the Volga Manufactory textile mill and son of Ivan Mindovsky, owner of the fine mansion by Kekushev on Povarskaya (see pp 69-74) which was also built by the same construction company. Unlike the Walcot villas, the Lazarev mansion, in a district dominated by early 19th century houses, is purely within the neo-classical milieu, one of the earliest in the neo-Empire style. It exhibits the usual plain ochre-coloured walls but it differs from them by the arrangement of interior space and the irregular, stylish exterior. The building is ingeniously designed in the shape of the letter J and the main entrance is not from the courtyard as it would be in a genuine Empire house but from the street at the bottom of the letter where it turns upwards. Originally it was of a single storey but a second floor was added after 1913. On the main corner where the two streets meet is a splendid rotunda of paired Tuscan columns identifying the beautiful round hall within. It is flanked by two dissimilar

loggias, also of Tuscan columns, which face two different streets and are not visible to each other giving an impression of disquiet quite opposed to the serenity of the true classical style. The mouldings so typical of Empire mansions appear here as incised reliefs in the loggias and rotunda. Inside, the house was divided into the living areas at the extreme ends, while the formal rooms were grouped around the magnificent rotunda hall and decorated with marble columns, wall paintings, parquet flooring of selected woods and elegant fireplaces.

After the revolution the owners were evicted and the mansion served for a time as the archive of the Red Army. In the 1920s it became the Embassy of Austria. In this capacity it has remained, and Austria is the only foreign country in Moscow to own its embassy outright. In the late 1930s after the Anschluss it reverted to Germany and it was probably in this building in 1939 that the notorious Molotov-Ribbentrop nonaggression pact between Germany and the Soviet Union was negotiated.

Gribov Villa

The area along Povarskaya Street, west of the Kremlin, was another fashionable district for the bourgeoisie. Here, among an enclave of neo-classical mansions, was the home of Vladimir Gribov, whose wealth, like the Morozovs' and Mindovskys' came from textile mills. The villa was built in 1909 by Alexei Miliukov (c. 1860-after 1915) and Boris Velikovsky (1878-1937) and is one of the most attractive houses in this

ABOVE

113 Lazarev, Mindovsky mansion, 1906;
the corner Tuscan rotunda flanked by the
loggia identifies the large circular hall
around which the house is organised.

OPPOSITE

114 Lazarev, apartment house on the Arbat, 1903:
a typical facade of the early Art Nouveau period
by an experienced architect who was to build the
Mindovsky mansion three years later.

117 Shekhtel s final house, 1909: although a two-storey
hall hides behind the Doric columns, the rustication,
sculptural reliefs and pediments reveal the inspiration
as Russian Empire of the early 1800s.

feet. Columns divide the rooms that are grouped around the hall; to the east is a charming oval room with a baroque ceiling and niches which protrudes into the garden. Vtorov was able to enjoy his new house for only five years. In 1918 he was shot there in mysterious circumstances but probably not by the Bolsheviks who allowed him a large public funeral, the last for the merchant class in the Soviet Union. Since 1933 the house has been the residence of the American Ambassador, 'Spaso House', and has been meticulously cared for.

Fyodor Shekhtel's House

The most vigorous of the neo-Empire houses is by any measure the last house the architect, Fyodor Shekhtel, built for himself (117). A two-storey villa, originally with a front garden out to the centre of the Garden Ring road, Bolshaya Sadovaya, it appears small and exposed today without the garden and in the shadow of later high-rise buildings all around. However, disregarding the surroundings, the unusual house is still most impressive. A severe Doric portico incised by three tall windows rises via a narrow pediment to the flat balustraded roof garden. Concealed behind the portico is a grand two-storey hall, almost a perfect cube, which is the centre of the house with its own staircase to the interior gallery. The bay to the right of the portico is divided neatly into the two floors, the prosaic ground floor and more important first floor with the elaborate window and balcony identifying the main bedroom. To the left, one

floor only is evident but this is balanced by the contiguous open archway under a relief of Athena and the muses which leads into the courtyard. The house extends well back and is more spacious than it would seem from the street. In the courtyard Shekhtel constructed a tall freestanding building as his studio. The underlying geometry of the house, the right angles, cubes and squares, so unlike the undulating forms of Art Nouveau, is evident

118 Zholtovsky, Gavril Tarasov's fortress, 1912: based on Palladio's Palazzo Thiene the heavily rusticated house of the Italian Renaissance is unique in Moscow.

119 Klein, Borodino bridge, 1912: the propylae gate marks the entrance to the severely classical bridge built to commemorate the Russian victory over the French in 1812.

the purges and shot as a Trotskyite in 1937. It eventually was taken over as headquarters of the secret police, the KGB, of the Krasnopresnensky district in Moscow. In 1992 they were obliged in their turn to leave to the regret of none and the house is being restored for use as an economic institute. It is hoped the rooms will return to something like their former state when it was Shekhtel's home.

Gavril Tarasov's Fortress

One singular mansion built in Moscow in these years was not based on Russian historical classicism but on the high peak of the Italian Renaissance. This is the Tarasov House, built in 1912 by Ivan Zholtovsky (1867-1959) (118), who was henceforth to remain true to his Italian inspiration and was to make a brilliant career in the 1930s to 1950s as master of Soviet neo-classicism. The heavily rusticated mansion with massive walls and rhythmically placed windows, more like an impenetrable fortress than a home, is an almost faithful copy of Palladio's Palazzo Thiene in Vicenza. The one exception is the greater emphasis given in the Zholtovsky building to the rusticated ground floor, thus enhancing the impression of a forbidding fortification. It forms a rectangle on a corner site flush with two streets completely enclosing a charming inner courtyard-garden in the Italian manner. Unlike Palladio's building where only two sides of the projected four were ever built, the Tarasov mansion completes the rectangle in full thereby entirely enclosing the inner garden.

at every turn. There is no mistaking the clever reworking of classical motifs – the columns, pediments, sculptural reliefs – with the imaginative organisation of space and volume to achieve an admirable translation of the old style into the new.

In 1918, Shekhtel and his family were obliged to leave their home and move into a series of communal apartments. The house and studio were occupied by artists and the house by among others Robert Eidemann, a Soviet hero of the civil war who was made director of the Frunze military academy but was caught up in

120 Rerberg, Kiev station, 1912-17: the classical facade facing the river contrasts sharply with the modern train shed behind.

The secret of the mansion lies within where the luxuriously appointed rooms and intimacy of the sheltered courtyard belie the cold, formidable exterior. Walls and marble fire-places left white or lightly coloured are offset by the heavily accented dark expanse of coffered ceilings decorated with paintings by Evgeny Lancere (1875-1946) and Ignaty Nivinsky (1881-1933). The interiors have survived well during its time as the Polish Embassy, and then the Institute of Africa and Asia, although some large, inappropriate African style murals have appeared in the stairwell.

The Tarasovs were merchants from cossack country in southern Russia who became highly successful traders in Moscow. The parsimonious brothers who founded the firm always travelled third class, carried all their victuals with them on long journeys, and wore the shabbiest of sheep-skin coats. The second generation were totally different. Gavril Gavrilovich, his name incised in Roman letters on the facade of his spectacular home, was certainly not opposed to showing off his wealth. His famous Moscow Renaissance home, poised as it was in the heart of bourgeois Moscow opposite the Morozov's Gothic pile and

121 Kiev station: the clock tower.

OPPOSITE
122 Klein, Pushkin Museum of Fine Art, 1912: the epitome in the revival of classicism displays Ionic columns and a fine frieze borrowed from the Acropolis.

just down the road from the Ryabushinsky's Art Nouveau house, was considered one of the wonders of the time. But the Tarasovs only enjoyed their splendid residence for five years; the family were obliged to emigrate to France in 1918 where one of their descendants, Henri Troyat, (Lev Tarasov) became a writer of biographies of Russian writers and novels about Russian history.

PUBLIC BUILDINGS
Classical Ensemble in Dorogomilovskoe

Not only private houses adopted the neo-classical style but great public buildings like museums and railway stations built in the 1910s at the end of the Moscow boom reflected the new taste. In western Moscow an unusual architectural ensemble of bridge and railway station echo the fashion for antique styles.

In honour of the centenary of the retreat of Napoleon from Moscow a memorial bridge, the Borodino, was built across the Moskva River, 1909-12, by the architect, Roman Klein (1858-1924), and engineer, N. Oskolkov (later to die in Stalin's camps). It linked the city with the suburban village of Dorogomilovskoe through which Napoleon and his army marched to seize Moscow after the battle of Borodino. Klein tackled the problem of the different heights of the banks, very low on the right, frequently flooded Dorogomilovskoe side, and high on the left, Moscow side, by two different solutions. On the low Dorogomilovskoe bank two tall obelisks incised with names of Russian officers in the 1812 war rise from round bastions flanking the commencement of the bridge. On the more built-up higher bank which gave access to Moscow proper Klein devised two curved elegant Doric propylaea also raised on bastions on either side of the bridge suggesting an entrance gate (119). The railings of the bridge are decorated with military insignia of the early 19th century. Today the twelve-storey buildings of the Soviet era which line the embankments on both sides render these gateways less effective and the impact they were designed to have on travellers entering and leaving the city was further diminished when the bridge was widened in 1952.

One of the last railway stations to be built before the revolution the Briansk (now Kiev) line running southwest to Kiev and the Ukraine and south-eastern Europe also exhibited the fashion for classicism (120). Designed by Ivan Rerberg (1869-1932) who had worked as an assistant with Klein, and Vyacheslav Oltarzhevsky (1880-1966), and built 1912-17 (interrupted by war and revolution and not finally completed until 1920), it was situated in a largely empty site after the draining of the embankment which was prone to flooding.

Its facade facing the river combines excellently with the classical lines of the Borodino bridge which is situated a little to the right of the station and serves to link it with the centre of the city. It is built on a frame of reinforced concrete which supports a magnificent train shed of glass and iron spanning forty-seven metres by Vladimir Shukhov, the remarkable engineer who twenty years earlier had fashioned the glass and metal roof of GUM.

Its modern functionalism, however, is belied by the fastidiously classical stone facade of the over-decorated archway entrances to the station surmounted by domes at each end and, between them, a long line of Ionic columns above the rusticated ground level. The inherent tedium of the facade is resolved, however, by the positioning of the tall elegant clock tower to the right which skillfully offsets the building (121). The later suburban line and metro station entrance added in the 1940s are discreetly placed behind the clock tower.

Pushkin Museum of Fine Art

The seminal classical building in Moscow before the First World War was the new national museum of fine art named for Alexander III, now the Pushkin Museum of Fine Art (122). It was built, 1898-1912, by the prolific architect, Roman Klein, who had over sixty buildings, mostly neo-classical, to his credit. He also made forays into the pseudo-Russian and even built a variation on Art Nouveau – the great Muir and Mirrielees Emporium, Moscow's first purpose-built department store, its modern construction and free internal arrangement hidden by clever Gothic cladding reflecting the founders' British origins. Klein's design for the Pushkin Museum was based on the winning entry to the competition of Pyotr Boitsov. It took fourteen years to complete because of constant uncertainties over funding and a fire in 1904.

The idea of such a museum of antique and medieval sculpture first arose in intellectual circles in the early 19th century but it was not until the appointment of Ivan Tsvetaev as Professor of the Chair of Fine Arts at the University of Moscow in the 1890s that it became a viable prospect. Professor Tsvetaev, whose daughter was the famous and tragic poetess, Marina Tsvetaeva, singlemindedly set out to realise his dream remaining undiscouraged by the incessant problems which beset him. In the end the project took twenty years of his life but he lived to witness the opening of the museum – he died a year later. He not only had to arrange for the collection of plaster casts of ancient

OPPOSITE
123 Pushkin Museum of Fine Art: upper gallery with the painting, *Dance*, by Henri Matisse.

fathers was more than matched by the imperial government which totally refused to make any donation at all. Tsvetaev was forced to turn to the wealthy merchants. Luckily, Varvara Alexeeva, a relative of Stanislavsky, willed a large sum at her death towards the cost of the museum making it possible to commence construction in 1898. But although other merchants and professional people like the architect Fyodor Shekhtel and Dr Zakharin made smaller donations of 20,000 rubles (the twenty-thousanders) the money coming in for the vast project was not sufficient. It was only when Tsvetaev met Yury Nechaev of St Petersburg that the problem was solved. Nechaev had unexpectedly inherited at the age of almost fifty a huge fortune from his bachelor uncle, Maltsev, whose only stipulation was that he add his uncle's name to his own. This windfall empowered Nechaev-Maltsev to indulge his life-long interest in intellectual pursuits in the realisation of the museum. He gave more than two million rubles in all in the long years the museum was under construction which enabled it to overcome day-to-day problems and avoid having to skimp on the fine materials and workmanship of the interiors, and the marble and stone cladding and superb sculpture of the facade.

It seems entirely appropriate that the museum of plaster casts of antique, medieval and Renaissance sculpture (it was only in 1924 that it acquired later European paintings) should be one of the most beautiful classical buildings in Moscow. Of two tall floors and a basement, set

sculptures from Greece and Italy, France and Britain, but he had to cut his way through the jungle of city politics to obtain a good position for the museum and, most difficult of all, he had to find all the money.

The city authorities in the end gave him an excellent position, a square block centrally situated on Volkhonka street not far from the Kremlin. Financial contributions were another matter, however, and the parsimony of the city

well back from the street and somewhat obscured by the ubiquitous fir trees that were planted in such profusion in front of Soviet official buildings, it exudes an air of serenity and stability. The Ionic portico of six columns inspired by the Erechtheum in the Athens Acropolis is flanked by long galleries of eight columns with a frieze of the Olympic games by the Petersburg sculptor, G. Zaleman. Above the portico is a copy of the Parthenon frieze sculpted by L. Armbruster and the high glass roof, also by the engineer Vlaldimir Shukhov, which provides excellent lighting for the exhibits. The richly appointed interior was fitted out with different halls (123): the Egyptian hall for the excellent collection of Vladimir Golenishchev which was acquired by the museum in 1909; the Greek hall designed like a courtyard with friezes and a temple, and the Italian or Medieval hall based on the Bargello Palazzo in Florence. The grand central staircase by Ivan Zholtovsky is edged with beautiful marble columns in a warm terracotta colour. The Pushkin Museum has certainly taken its place as one of the great art museums of the world with its unique collection not only of plaster casts but of paintings including Rembrandt and Goya, and French art including the leading impressionists, all culled from private collections before the revolution. It was also the venue for the 1996-97 exhibition of the Treasures of Troy, the priceless Troy gold that had been taken from the Berlin museum by Soviet troops in 1945 and hidden from view for over thirty years.

INHERITORS OF ART NOUVEAU

Thus Art Nouveau had played out its contribution by 1910 and was superseded by what seemed a retrograde movement, the return to the certainties of classical architecture at a time of increasing political tension. It seemed that the innovations and new ideas generated by Art Nouveau only a decade earlier had disappeared without trace. But this was not so. As is evident above, the new ways of treating

ABOVE AND OPPOSITE
124 Melnikov, the architect s own house, 1929: the most original of the constructivist architecture of the 1920s is this double-cylinder house of the gifted Konstantin Melnikov.

space within buildings introduced by the architects of Art Nouveau were also adopted by the designers of neo-classicism. And the technological advances so enthusiastically embraced at the beginning of the century continued to be applied to buildings which otherwise resembled those of a century earlier in Moscow. In other words, the neo-classical houses and buildings were to some extent merely facades, hiding the modern building within.

Where was architecture to go from there? The neo-classical style like Art Nouveau before it seemed inappropriate as the war with Germany loomed and political and social conflict intensified. (Some of the most successful architects with German names, like Shekhtel, had a bad time in the war in spite of the centuries their families had lived in Russia; Shekhtel's son, Lev, felt it prudent to adopt his mother's more Russian maiden name, Zhegin). Architecture was of course in abeyance during the war years except for those buildings started before the conflict. After the war was over, the old world of Russia no longer existed and a revolutionary government with an entirely new agenda had taken over. Architecture along with the other arts could not but reflect the new situation. The visual arts in particular formed a synthesis in the early years of the Bolshevik government, painters, sculptors, and architects working together in the new studios and workshops boldly experimenting in avant-garde design. Unlike the arts and crafts movement at Abramtsevo forty years earlier, the machine-age was warmly embraced, and

functionalism became the central principle around which a new, revolutionary style of art was devised. In architecture this led to constructivism in which the bare bones of buildings were revealed, in which ornamentation was reduced to almost nothing, and form was the guiding light. Beauty was to be expressed in the sheer geometry of the building.

Some exceedingly original and ingenious buildings were erected in the 1920s in Moscow in the fervour of this new philosophy which rival the products of the parallel movement in Germany at the Bauhaus. To this day these buildings exhilarate by the purity of line and utter originality of form. Anyone who has seen and explored the wonderfully innovative house by Konstantin Melnikov (1890-1974), in the form of two inter-locking cylinders (124), on Staroarbatsky Pereulok, cannot but be convinced that Russia was at the forefront of this movement.

The playful experiments with shape and volumes of the early Art Nouveau houses like Shekhtel's Ryabushinsky or Derozhinskaya mansions or Kekushev's Mindovsky house matured into a more refined pared-down style reflected in the commercial premises such as Erikhson's printing house or Shekhtel's *Utro Rossii* building or his wonderful Merchants' Trading Society building. From these examples it can be seen that the lessons learned in the heyday of Art Nouveau were simply reapplied in a more rigorous fashion in the 1920s when for a short but exceedingly fertile time experiment and originality were encouraged in architecture.

This functionalism was quickly brushed aside as Stalin tightened his hold in the 1930s and a rigid authority was once more imposed on Russian society. The neo-classicism favoured in the harshest years of Stalin's dictatorship parallels the return to the Empire style in the last years of the reign of Nicholas II; to both regimes however opposite in ideology, the monumentality and certainty of classical architecture as the officially approved style largely appealed as a reflection of the sure rock on which they believed their regimes were built. Here the west except for fascist Germany did not follow or lead. Although between the wars Art Deco became fashionable it was never a servile reflection of classical architecture but a modern variant and a precursor to the international modern of the post-war years. In Russia international modern was also adopted for economic rather than aesthetic reasons some years after Stalin's death. It is only now, after long decades of hostility and neglect, that the refreshingly different style of Art Nouveau that so captivated Moscow at the beginning of the century, is being appreciated again and its contribution to the development of modern architecture is being properly evaluated.